OUTSIDE THE BOX

Warren,
Thank you for all
your encouragement.

OUTSIDE THE BOX

NINE ENTREPRENEURIALLY-MINDED COLLEGE
STUDENTS WHO FOLLOWED THEIR INSTINCTS
AND DISCOVERED THEIR LIFE'S PASSION

Robert Bloch

Champlain Publishing ▸▸

Champlain Edition
First printing November 2011

IBSN 978-0-9834292-3-4

Cover Design by Kaitlyn Bouchard

Interior Layout and Design by Jordan LaCount

For information on Champlain Publishing, see ChamplainCollegePublishing.com

To the many wonderful young people I have had the opportunity to work with in my time at Champlain College, who have taught me so much and have given me boundless optimism about the future.

And to my grandson, Owen Robert Doyle, the "O'dawg."

INTRODUCTION RB

Sometimes I think I am the luckiest person in the world. Every day I get to work with some of the brightest, most optimistic and interesting young people around—student entrepreneurs and would-be entrepreneurs at Champlain College, most of whom have participated in the college's innovative entrepreneurship education program, BYOBiz (Bring Your Own Business).

Every week during the school year, one or two new students come to see me, filled with ideas, dreams, and enthusiasm for the life that lies ahead. You can feel their eager anticipation for what they will find around the next corner or with the next question they ask. They have so much to learn and they know it—but they are undaunted, they see the possibilities, and you can just feel the energy they exude.

Unlike a traditional professor, who might see a student twice a week for fifteen weeks during a semester-long course, I work with many of these students over a number of years; I get to share their ups and downs and see them struggle, fail, triumph, grow, and mature. It's a gas!

How did I get so lucky? That's a long story, but here's the short version. A little over four years ago I was at a career impasse. After two extended entrepreneurial ventures, one quite successful, the other not so much, I was trying to buy another company—my third venture in about 15 years. It wasn't going well. The company was imploding as we were negotiating and—right at the brink of becoming emotionally involved with the deal (always dangerous)—I made the difficult decision to pull the plug.

So there I was, at age 57, with nothing to do. I found myself asking, "Do you really want to do another one of these 'Let's build a company' gigs?" I knew right away that if you even find yourself asking that question, the answer is no. Building a company more or less from scratch is so demanding, in every respect, that you really do have to have both passion and commitment.

I found myself examining my previous career experience: my 17 years in marketing management as well as my entrepreneurial experience. I even foraged through some long-forgotten boxes in my basement and dug out the notes from a course I had taken at Harvard Business School called Self Assessment and Career Development. In all this, I was searching for some useful themes that could guide me. Specifically, what was I doing, and with

whom, and how did I relate to those around me when I was happiest in my work?

This task was made more difficult by the simple fact that I enjoyed so much of my working life—it was almost all good. But I did come up with a few themes, one of which was that I was particularly happy and satisfied in my work when I was mentoring and developing younger managers. But what does one do with that? I thought about teaching—I think I never had met a teacher, at any level, who didn't truly love it. On the other hand, I had also heard that academia was one of the slowest-moving and most politically charged work environments. That seemed so alien to me. Could I be happy in such an environment?

All that conjecture faded away when I heard about a unique opportunity at Champlain College, a small college in Burlington, Vermont known for professionally oriented academic programs. The College was looking for the first full-time director of its new entrepreneurship program, BYOBiz. I didn't know much about the college, but from living in the community for a while, I did know that Champlain enjoyed an excellent reputation as an innovative, nimble entrepreneurial institution, so I interviewed for the position. The outcome: Champlain liked me and I really liked Champlain, so off we went!

This book tells some of the stories of student entrepreneurs I have worked with since then, through interviews I conducted during the fall of 2011. They tell their stories, share their successes, failures, what they were thinking, and what they learned–about entrepreneurship and about themselves.

In many ways, these are not just stories about kids starting their own businesses. They're coming-of-age stories. They are stories about kids who, by starting a business, found a passion, a sense of purpose, and started a lifelong journey. Whether these early ventures ended up making some money or not, the kids discovered a new, creative dimension to themselves that will now be a part of who they are for the rest of their lives.

It is my hope that other student entrepreneurs— or entrepreneurs at all stages of life, for that matter—can benefit and find inspiration from the experiences and insights shared here by these remarkable young people.

I hope you enjoy these interviews as much as I have.

"You never know what you have unless you actually try to make it something."

SLAM DUNK Alex Brandstetter

International Business '10 | Hometown: Derby, VT | Passion: Marketing | Entourage Marketing Group

Alex Brandstetter is an articulate, self-possessed, passionate young man. Like most of the entrepreneurs in this book, he is a person of many talents and interests, so unsurprisingly there are many dimensions to his story.

Like many of our interviewees, Alex tells a story that involves a great deal more than just how he began his own business—or businesses, as he has now graduated college and is building his own marketing company. It's a story about how he discovered who he really is. In fact, any young entrepreneur is really in the business of discovering who he or she is.

One aspect of Alex's story in particular that I find interesting is his struggle, as he approaches adulthood, to break away from his family identity and forge his own. This is a process all teens go through; it's part of growing up. The interesting dimension of Alex's struggle is not that he is trying to escape an unfortunate background, but trying to establish his own identity, credentials and value, rather than simply ride the coattails of his rather famous and accomplished family.

When did you first get an inkling that you might want to do something entrepreneurial?

I think that right from the beginning, in my first job, I got to see the level of freedom that my superiors had in running their own business, and that really interested me.

My first job was at a country club in Newport, Vermont. I probably called myself the assistant pro back then but I was really more of the pro's assistant.

As the pro's assistant, what did you do?

Well, I stocked the pro shop, did a lot of customer service, made sure people were getting out on the tee, made sure that the members were happy. It was really like a PR job. Obviously there was a lot of grunt work like washing cars, washing clubs, caddying, stuff like that; but as I grew in that pro shop I got more responsibility. I got to teach lessons—but the interesting thing is that when you work at a country club you meet a lot of business people. You meet a lot of executives, you meet a lot of professionals in

general, so I think that I grew up around these big ideas and these people with these big ideas that made contributions to my town, and I think that subconsciously, I was always motivated by being in that crowd.

What was the first big decision that the pro, your boss, let you make yourself?

I remember it to this day. The first decision that he let me make was a new way to organize the pro shop—the layout of the merchandise. He sent me out to the hardware store. I built my own racks and I stained everything and I made sure it was presented in the way I knew he would like—but the freedom he gave me to make those decisions was huge for me at that age.

How old were you then?

I was probably 16, 17 years old. He sent me down to the shop, he gave me a budget, and I built him a new pro shop layout. People loved it. The reception was awesome. I don't know if it led to more sales or what, but the fact that he let me come up with the idea for the new pro shop layout was a big undertaking at that age. I think that was also the year that he started to leave me in the pro shop myself more often, and I got to run the show. That point was when he started to look at me more as an assistant pro. So at 17, 18, I was working for him and we actually built a good team.

And what did your parents think of all this as they saw you developing in this way?

Both my parents were proud; I was proud of myself to see that I had a job at such an early age. Actually, ever since I was legally allowed to work, I've held a job and I think my parents are also proud of that.

They always told me that I would never find a job at which I could play golf all day, right? Because I used to love golf, and they always thought that a good job would be landscaping, where you're dirty, and put some blood, sweat, and tears into your job. But I lucked out; I got to dress up everyday, I got to hang out with the cool business people in town, I got to shoot the shit with some of the big influencers in Northeast Vermont. They all came to the golf course and I knew everybody on a first name basis, so I really lucked out, as a kid, to have that job.

That must have given you a lot of self-confidence, interacting with all those guys.

Absolutely. I had a competitive advantage also because I played golf better than a lot of them, so they were always looking to me for advice on their golf game, and I think that it made for a good conversation, to start learning more about what they do for a living, and just to be in their frame of mind. It made me mature a little bit to hold a conversation with these adults. You can't be a kid when you're trying to teach an architect how to play golf, so it made me grow up and made me change my lingo, and I think that it made me more approachable.

So you're 16, 17, you're probably thinking about college; what were you thinking about as your logical next step?

Well, at that time I was really interested in not only golf, but also interested in architectural design, so my first college was Vermont Technical College, going for Architectural Engineering. One of the connections I made at the golf course was an architect so he actually let me intern in his office and I became a draftsman, and I loved that as well. I thought that golf was more of a hobby than a profession, so I was really interested in architecture and I think that today I really have that design knack; I think that even if you look at how the pro let me design his pro shop and build the furniture—I think that was from my knack to be a little bit more design oriented.

So you go to Vermont Tech and you study Architectural Engineering. But then you made a shift because obviously you came to Champlain where there's no architecture and there's no engineering!

I think I was missing the business side of things. Obviously if you're an architect, you're running a business if you're running your own firm, but I think that for me, I wanted to contribute more from a marketing point of view. While I was working for this architect, yeah, I was being a draftsman, but I was pitching ideas on how to get more business because he was not really bringing in a ton. He had a good business up in my neck of the woods, but I always was thinking, "Let's get more business. Let's grow."

I always had the mentality of pitching the business, reeling customers in, letting it grow, so I had a need to learn more about marketing and I think that's why I transferred to Champlain.

And I also think I grew and I changed. At that age it's hard to tell someone who's so creative and so interested in so many different things what they want to do for a living. I chose architectural engineering because at that time, that's what I liked, but I think that for me, marketing was more of an occupation that I could thrive in.

That's interesting. Back then, to the extent that you were even aware of something called marketing, what did it mean to you?

Well, my family owns Bogner, an international designer ski clothing company and brand, so I've always had an idea of marketing and promo materials and branding. I tried to apply those to the small businesses I was working at.

So all during your childhood, it was more like everyone was talking about it in your family and it was sort of osmosis?

It was osmosis, but it was also that my dad would come home with marketing materials as gifts for us. Point-of-purchase stuff that really doesn't mean that much, just maybe a logo that's carved out of a piece of wood or something, stuff to sell product. He would come home with stuff from last season and give it to us, and we would decorate our bedrooms with it. So I always had stuff laying around—posters and logos and just random stuff to promote business. I didn't know that that was marketing at the time, or advertising, but that's what tweaked me: coming

up with these different ways of promoting a business.

At the time were they thinking that you'd go into the family business at some point?

My dad was never really a big fan of nepotism, but I definitely was very proud of my family's company and felt somewhat tied to it because I grew up around it. I used to run through the factory where my dad worked, and I didn't really picture my life without that company being in it, but as I grew up I became a little more independent. It's great to have it as a crash landing pad, but I never wanted to succumb to that. I wanted to make my career take off on its own.

My dad's side of the family is very, very successful in that industry. They are renowned in Germany and in Europe—they're just a very successful group of people. My mom's side of the family is also a very successful group of people and I kind of found myself in the middle, always name dropping each side; I never really was myself. I was related to these people, and as I got older, I thought that it was more of a crutch than anything. When you're younger, you sort of use that as a defense mechanism, and when I got older I started to feel almost embarrassed that the only card I had in my hat was these relationships that really didn't mean shit for me. I didn't make these accomplishments, I don't work for this company, I didn't come up with these ideas; I'm just related to them.

Do you think that was in any way a motivator for you in some way to prove yourself?

Absolutely. That was, I think, a personal motivator. Not like I woke up every morning saying, "Screw this company; I'm going to do my own thing." It wasn't that. I think it was just this little constant reminder: make your own name, do your own thing, and make your own living. You should be proud that you don't need them.

So when you were in the golf shop and you started to get a little recognition doing something of your own, that had a lot of meaning for you?

It did, because my entire family golfs, and I was probably the best golfer in the family, so I'd kind of already made my name in that. But then, not only was I a good golfer, I was able to turn it into a revenue driver for myself. I was bringing money in. I didn't need an allowance; I was able to make somewhat of a living at that age.

That's fascinating. So you're at Champlain, you're in international business, as I remember, and then something happened, right? I'm talking about the Slam for Sudan.

My first year at Champlain I was in an International Marketing class and we were talking about things like international issues and entering foreign markets. We were broken up into teams and assigned a company to work for, or work with, to come up with a marketing proposal.

The company we were paired with was actually a non-profit called the Global Reach Partnership. Tom Myers and Scott Baker, both professors at Champlain, started this non-profit to support new Americans, more specifically the Sudanese refugees in Burlington, helping them learn vocational skills, getting them on their feet.

The Sudanese come from a horrific background of genocide. They were the survivors who had walked through Africa to safety. Those of them who came to America were nicknamed "The Lost Boys" because they raised themselves, like the Lost Boys in Peter Pan. They needed a lot of support and we were essentially paired with them to create a marketing plan to raise awareness, raise money, and focus on their culture.

The first thing we knew we had to do was create a plan for an event. Obviously, my background was golf so I thought this would be a cool way to have a golf tournament where a bunch of rich, WASP-y guys go out there and play golf and donate the winnings to the cause. But I knew that wouldn't resonate with the Sudanese community at all.

The next and more obvious suggestion was a basketball tournament. Almost immediately, the little phrase that popped into my head was "Slam for Sudan." I'd noticed that Vermont does not have a slam-dunk contest for kids. They have the playoffs and finals at the high school level, but nothing to really focus on their specific individual talents.

A dunk is a rare occurrence in a Vermont basketball court, but a lot of the kids are able to do it, so I thought it would be fun to put on a dunk contest, where Vermonters don't typically get to see that in high school games. I was pretty confident that it would be a success and I know that kids amongst themselves have dunk contests in practice, so I thought that they would be amped up to be a part of it. I had no idea how successful that idea would actually be.

So you did it as a class assignment, where you wrote it up as a paper, you handed it in, you got your grade—but then something happened and you did more than that.

The class was only a semester long, so how many months is that? Three months? Four months? And it was supposed to be purely hypothetical, right? It was supposed to be for a grade: come up with an idea, make a marketing plan proposal, pitch it to the company and get a grade. But in this case, our assignment was twenty-six pages long, which was ten pages longer than the assignment and it was so flawlessly planned out that it really was actionable. It could have happened.

We were paired with a non-profit that really needed a lot of help, and I thought personally that it would be a slap in the face to just take a grade for this project and go on to the next semester. I thought that we had something more to contribute, and I pitched this idea to the team.

The student team that worked on the project?

Yes, the student team. There were four of us at that time. I said, "Let's see this come to fruition," and I kind of made them feel a little guilty also, like, "How can you just take a grade for this? I mean, they can potentially make a lot of money with this idea."

I've always been a little bit of a free-spirit type of motivational speaker and I've always tried to motivate my basketball teams and all that, so I think I was able to influence them to take part, and they gave 110 percent. That's how we built the team initially; we just recruited all of our friends from all the different majors to come in and contribute their skills. Essentially we were running a little business. By the end of it, the team went from the four of us to more than 30 people. We had a marketing department, we had an accounting department...

Web designers?

Yep, we had a web team and we had people running out getting sponsors. We had budgets. With the money we brought in from sponsors, we had to pay our expenses. We had to pay for the gym, for the T-shirts for kids, and the list of expenses goes on. We had to be profitable in order to make them some money, so we had tight budgets, obviously.

Our biggest expense was the gym. We were looking for a main sponsor to cover that and we found three: The Vermont Frost Heaves professional basketball team, Ben & Jerry's and Bogner, my parents' company, helped. So we found those three initial sponsors and we put their logos out and showed it to other potential sponsors. The donor confidence of having those brands associated with our event just had the money pour in. We had a ton of donations. I don't know the amount we had—it was just a perfect storm.

What were your biggest challenges in pulling this thing off?

I think the biggest challenges were to get the team to buy in completely. We're all dreamers to some extent, but eventually you have to look at the dream and say, is the juice worth the squeeze? I think the hardest part for me was motivating them constantly. Not that I felt that they would slack off, I just felt it was required, to show them the progress we've been making over time, and some days there was nothing really to present so I had to fiercely come up with new ways to keep them motivated and on the mission.

You obviously had a passion for this. You had a team of twenty, thirty kids working on this, right?

Yeah. How do you motivate that many people with so many different priorities? How do you keep them on the same wavelength? And a lot of the people, they respect you if you bring ideas to the table and if you actually pursue them on your own. If you're just delegating or dictating to them what to do, and you do nothing, you're just the manager, I don't think that really drives a lot of teams—it's not really a team builder. So we definitely found that we had to put our own elbow grease in. Nobody was going to do it for us, and I think that that behavior led the other teammates to contribute more, because they knew that we were not just in it for the glory, that we were actually contributing.

It obviously was a big success. How much did you gross on this thing?

We netted $6,500, but between in-kind donations and cash donations, we grossed about $14 grand.

And you had the 400 people in the gym...

No, I think there were six, seven hundred. We

had a lot of fundraising fodder to entice people to come in. Shearer Chevrolet gave us a Chevy Malibu Hybrid for somebody to take a three-point shot for and the kid almost made it.

Yeah, I remember that. That's a great story. And then the next year another team carried on with it.

Yeah. It's always hard to have a sequel because there are a lot of expectations. We had a new team, a lot of the kids that contributed the most the first year were not back, and there were some other events that were going on in Burlington that day, but we still made a profit and we still donated money to the Global Reach Partnerships. It was a great event.

So in the wake of that, what was the next chapter?

The next chapter was taking the team that we had built for the first Slam for Sudan and saying, "We worked so well together and we had so much fun making these marketing materials, these posters, these websites, we came up with

ads, we were on the radio, we were on TV, we came up with all this material to promote this event—why don't we start our own marketing agency?"

Obviously, this is not the best economy to take that big of a risk, so it's been a slow progress, but we're still in it. We have a website, we're getting traffic and I think that when we find ourselves in more of a place to take a risk, we might invest a little more time and money into the project, but we know that we work well together, we know we want to work for ourselves and we're just waiting for the right time.

And what's your agency specialize in? Marketing's a very broad topic.

We specialize in small business branding. When small businesses need marketing help, they are often deterred by these huge agency retainers. It's very scary for a small business to invest that much into marketing, when it really is hard to track the return on it. So we said, "Why don't we do it in house? We don't charge for our creative, because that's objective, we charge by the hour, and let's grow this thing on a very transparent business model that people can really buy into."

We want to become part of their organization. We want to become part of their marketing. We don't want to be just some sideshow that builds a bunch of stuff, spits it out on them and then say, "It's your turn to grow. We did our work."

We actually want to become part of their team. That's why we called ourselves Entourage; we want to become part of their branding, advertising, marketing entourage. We felt that was a great business strategy and a lot of people like it. We've done some work for Peggy Fleming, the Olympic gold medal-winning figure skater. She was a great client. We did work for Heritage Flight [the aircraft charter and fixed based operator for private aircraft and jets at Burlington Airport]—we did some concept ads for them. We also did some work for some more local businesses, such as a hair salon start-up in Stowe that now has one of the largest men's hair salon shops in the area. We did all of her branding; we basically set up her color scheme so now she has a theme that's really something

people resonate with and she's pretty successful. I'd like to say it's because of our marketing but we choose our clients carefully; we want to make sure that it's a team.

Interesting. And what, when you reflect back, what was the toughest obstacle that you had to overcome?

I've always dealt with an Attention Deficit Disorder (ADD) that really made learning a chore for me; I never excelled at it. I always needed special attention, needed teachers to give me special treatments, and school was always hard for me to enjoy. A lot of kids go through it with flying colors but for me it was one of the hardest times of my life and for my parents also.

When I was younger I was medicated for this, and I think that the biggest challenge lately has been to drop the medication and do it on my own, find my own strategies and methods on how to focus and how to stay productive. That's been a huge trial for me, but I think what I'm learning is it's also giving me more confidence. It's making me learn techniques and tactics on how to be as productive as possible without the use of a medication and I feel like it's just making me a better all around person, socially and professionally.

Where do you see yourself in ten years?

I'm trying to live in the now. I'm trying to take it one day at a time right now because it's hard to plan that far ahead, especially with the way the economy is. You must just cherish that you have a job and that you have income—but in ten years I would love to see myself running my own company. I would love to see myself being independent. Eventually I want to get to a point where I can look and say, "I support myself. I don't need the support of an employer." I want to contribute my own ideas, make my own decisions, but right now I find myself in a really good spot; I've got a great job and they are listening to my ideas and I'm contributing.

What advice would you have for a teenager now who's maybe wondering about this whole entrepreneurship thing?

If you have an idea, you have to actually put the work behind it to see it come to life. And it's so rewarding to see an idea come from conception to reality. I would strongly encourage anyone who has an idea, who's been thinking about it for a considerable amount of time to just jump in with both feet and give it a shot. And if it doesn't work out, maybe it's not the right idea and maybe it spurs other ideas and things will evolve—but don't just sit there and have ideas and don't contribute because it's really a waste of time and a waste of energy just to let these things evaporate. You never know what you have unless you actually try to make it something.

Alex is a true leader. He has drive, an incredible amount of energy, and the ability to infect everyone around him with the same qualities.

Another dimension about Alex is his instinct to mine the most value and experience from whatever situation he is in—to see opportunity where others see nothing. This is an important characteristic of most successful entrepreneurs.

He manages to make the most of every opportunity to try things, learn skills, meet people. He did it in what could be a fairly mundane summer job at a golf course, where he convinced his boss to let him redesign the entire pro shop. That pro shop was the source of much of his boss's income—a big responsibility for a teenager.

Then Alex transformed a classroom assignment into the opportunity to create and lead a fairly large organization that was trying to perform a fairly complex task–staging a successful show and fundraiser. Again, most people would have just been happy to get the class assignment out of the way, but Alex perceived a much bigger opportunity and bigger potential reward. Not only was he successful in raising money for Global Reach Partnerships, but he and his team also got first-hand experience with the skills necessary for business. They had to learn logistics, marketing, branding, sponsorship, web design, community-building, budgeting—almost everything a young entrepreneur needs to learn.

And now, he's doing the same in his marketing company. Whereas most marketing companies charge for each project by what's produced for the client based on the perceived value, which is honestly very difficult to accurately calculate, Alex saw the potential for a different system that is much more tangible and comfortable for clients to invest in. Alex, like any successful entrepreneur, identified a need for change in his market and used his skill set and connections to create his venture.

Alex consistently extracts the most experiential value for himself, and thereby accelerates his personal growth exponentially. He gets his hands on an idea, does the dirty work to make it happen—and it pays off. And that feels good.

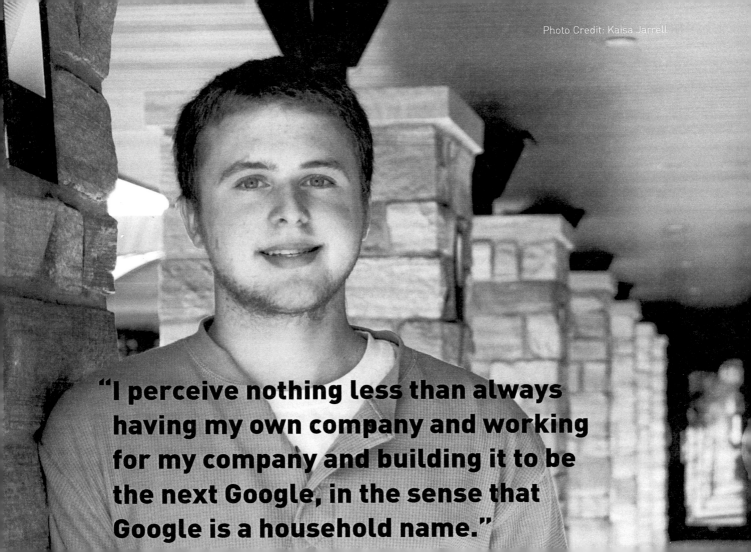

Photo Credit: Kaisa Jarrell

"I perceive nothing less than always having my own company and working for my company and building it to be the next Google, in the sense that Google is a household name."

MY HOBBY IS NICKO Nick Foley

Business '14 | Hometown: Northborough, MA | Passion: Business | Nicko Lawn Care

If you were to meet Nick Foley walking across campus, a big smile on his face, tossing off "How ya doin'?" and "How's it goin'?" to nearly everyone, dressed as he usually is in his shorts, high top sneakers, T-shirt, with a scruffy beard, you might conclude he's a typical college sophomore. Probably the last thing you might think is that he's also a seasoned entrepreneur who—from his dorm in Vermont—runs a profitable business in Massachusetts that racks up close to $100,000 a year in sales.

As Nick tells his story, you can feel him struggle to balance his life as an entrepreneur, which he truly loves and values, with the pressures to be like everyone else on campus, and to balance the demands of a thriving business with the other demands of a young life—studies, hanging out with and being accepted by friends.

Nick, when was the first time you had an interest in business or in having your own business? What was happening, where were you, what was it all about, what got you inspired?

When I was in the second grade, my brother and my friend from down the street—they're older than me—were very mechanically inclined. They liked to play in the sandbox, and they were always playing around with tractors.

One day we just walked over to my neighbor's house, and asked her if she wanted her lawn mowed for $15, and we split it $5 three ways. My brother and friend went out and got their $5 for mowing the lawn, and I got my $5 for doing the paperwork, talking to her and billing her, things like that.

It seemed to work out really well because, if you ever meet my brother, you'll find he'll do whatever he can to not have to talk to you. He just hates dealing with the customers, so we were a good match for each other. He could do the work and I could handle the customers.

As a second grader, was it cool to run a business, make money? Were you guys proud of it?

Every year we would say, "This is the last year. We can't do this any more," just because we thought we'd be embarrassed. Like the other kids would think it's weird to be mowing lawns. I remember clear as day saying, "Okay, we're going to middle school—we can't be mowing lawns." We all said that: "We're going into middle school—we can't be doing this." And then, "We're in high school now—we can't be doing this."

High school was where I realized, yes, we can be doing this, because we're making money, and we like doing it. But every single year for the first five years, maybe even the first eight years, the famous quote would be, "This is the last year. We're done with this. We don't want to do this anymore."

What was going on there? Was it embarrassment, like "It's not what the cool kids are doing"?

That was exactly it.

But you were kind of cool in a way because you had money, and probably a lot of your friends didn't, right?

No, we didn't like doing it because it would just come across as weird, I guess. I'm not really sure. Because I do remember, even in the early days, we would stick flyers on telephone poles, or put them in mailboxes, as opposed to mailing them. We would go to all the streets around my house, but we would avoid our friends' houses, where we knew the people. Just because we thought it would be awkward. The average kid wants to do what every kid is doing, and not do something different.

So what kept you going and kept you doing it? What was it that turned you on and gave you whatever the motivation?

I wish I could say it was the money, but that motivation seems to not have kicked in yet.

Now you mentioned right from the get-go, your brother got $5 for doing the lawn, your friend got $5 for doing the lawn, and you got $5 for doing the paperwork. So right from there you were the executive. And your brother's older?

Yeah, he's older than me. If you were to follow us around for a day, you would see, even though it's my company, Jimmy is more or less the boss. I'll plan out our day, like we're going to go out and mow these lawns and mulch here, and he'll be like, "No, no, no, we're going to do this, that, and the other thing," just because he's older, and the older brother generally always has the last word. The only reason that it's named after me and I'm the owner is because he didn't want to talk to the customers.

Well, I've heard you on the phone, and you were very good. So maybe that was a smart decision for you guys.

I do like it, and plus, I just know, if I'm mowing, it's not going come out as good if my brother were to do it. I just prefer not to do it, because he's going do it better.

So in between you and your brother, who's more the entrepreneur?

Definitely me.

So he's sort of the chief operating officer, but you're the driving force.

Yes. I perceive nothing less than just always having my own company and working for my company and building it to be the next Google, in the sense that Google is a household name. Next it's going to be Nicko. Whereas my brother's always trying to tell me, "Sell it and cash out now. Sell it while you can." And I see no point in getting rid of it.

So you're the positive force, and he's sort of the cautious force.

Yeah. Like if we take jobs, someone will call me up and be like, "Oh, do you install patios?" And we generally don't install patios, but we have done it before, so I would say, "Yes, that's something we can look into." But he would be like, "No, we can't do that at all. We can't do that."

So without a doubt you are the entrepreneur. This is very interesting. So where do you think your positive energy or positive attitude comes from?

I don't know. Sometimes I'll get really stressed out, and I'll think, "Why am I doing this? Why am I spending my time at college running this business and not having all the college fun like everyone else?"

That whole time some of the other kids here are sitting there enjoying playing *Skate*, for example, on Xbox, I'm thinking, I have to call that lady, and I don't want to call her because she's going to complain about this or that. And I've got to call this other person to explain that maybe I was wrong on that invoice and maybe their payment got lost in the mail. Or I have to call someone else and explain that maybe I told them yesterday we were going to be there today, but I have to tell them today that we're not going to be there until tomorrow. And you just don't want to sit there and call these people, because as nice as everyone is, you're not a kid to them, you're the person on the other end of the phone who works for a company. It's serious business.

You're not a kid.

Exactly.

When did you first feel in your role as a businessperson that you're not a kid to your customers?

To be completely honest, even right now if I were to go and knock on a door and talk to a customer, I would feel as if I'm a kid, because I get a certain kind of look.

So they see you face-to-face and say, "Oh he's a kid," and you feel like a kid. Over the phone you're Mr. Foley. When you were, say, in eighth grade, if you got on the phone, did you get that feeling that they thought you were a kid, or did they take you as a serious businessperson?

Going into high school we had something like 25 lawns—which is really nothing compared to your average landscape company, but for a kid still in middle school that's pretty good. Those first

25 customers knew exactly who I was and they knew we were kids. Now we have hundreds of people who somehow know of us, whether we've done their property before or they get a mailing, or they heard online, so they think of us as a company.

Interesting. So if you don't mind me asking, how much did your business gross this past year?

Last year, when I was in high school, we did around $57,000 gross revenue, and I thought that was really good. And I was thinking, okay, I think I can double that during freshman year at Champlain. We ended up only doing over $85,000 this year. Which is still very good, and very profitable.

That's about 60 percent growth, which is pretty good.

We really doubled in growth every year up until the last few years. The first year we had two, our neighbor and this other lady, June, who lived two streets over. The next year we had four, and then eight, and then sixteen. So it really seemed to come very close to doubling each year. But I must say, if I had gone to a different college where my business wasn't one of my top priorities, I don't think I'd be where I am now. Even then, I still don't feel that freshman year was good for business.

You couldn't focus?

Yeah. And then I would stress out about possibly not taking advantage of my first year of college. I have the rest of my life to make money and run a business, but I only have one year to be a freshman in college. Midway through freshman year I remember being like, "Wow, I feel like I went back in time."

So you had 60 percent growth, but you feel like you neglected the business.

Exactly.

Do you know how many people would give a lot to be in that situation?

Yeah, but how many businessmen, maybe 50

years old right now, would give even more to go back to their freshman year and have a great time? So I have justified it to myself, I guess. I don't feel regret.

My point is that if you're feeling disappointed about 60 percent growth while you're still trying to have this other expansive part of your life...

Yeah, I do feel much better now, but I just felt like I could have done a lot more with the business given the resources here. I more or less neglected some opportunities. But that's also what made me be okay, by not pushing the business too hard.

So, you struggled during your freshman year to find a balance between the opportunities of your business and the opportunities of being at college. Given that experience, how do you see yourself managing that balance during the remainder of your college years?

I'm going to use a lot more of the resources here

until I graduate in 2014, not necessarily to have a very successful short term landscaping business, but to set the foundation for something larger; I'm just going to expand what I have put in place and hopefully go from there.

What do you feel you have learned by owning and running Nicko?

I feel that the past 10 years have taught me not necessarily how to run a business, but how not to run a business. For example, we used to send three people out to mow: my brother, my friend who started with us, and then my other friend we hired just for the silly reason that "I can't just not send you out to work, as if I don't want you to not make any money." I was Mister Nice Guy. I probably would not have sent out so many people to do work. I probably would have been more like my dad since day one. He always said, "Have a system. The only thing that separates McDonald's from all the other businesses like them is that they have a system. So come up with that." I just never really sat down and wrote down what to do. If I were to disappear tomorrow, I

don't think someone would be able to run Nicko. So I regret not doing all that stuff, but then at least when I start now after I graduate, I will know everything that I need to do.

If I could go back in time 10 years, I'd have twice as much of everything, whether it would be money in the bank, or equipment, or customers, because I know what not to do.

Well, you have a system now. I know we have talked about how you wanted to upgrade it, and build more infrastructure...

No, Dad was talking about literally having a three ring binder full of pieces of paper.

Policies and procedures, where everything is documented. Now, you mentioned your father. What was your father's influence in all this?

Well, he works for himself as a contractor. He builds houses and other structures. He has been very helpful, and he's always really encouraging. He wants me to do whatever makes sense to progress the company. But it's not really the typical father-son thing.

You're rebelling against him?

Not exactly. The majority of the time he helps me out. For example, he lets me use his truck whenever I need to use it. Or even now customers are sending me payments to my house and Dad puts them in another envelope and mails them up to me—things like that. And he's also gone out with me to a job and helped me do the work when I was stuck.

But he also tries to give me advice all the time to the point where I feel like, "Okay, it's the same thing over and over again." But it definitely does help. He was always big into having a system and being organized and having procedures so that one day you can move forward, so it's not a question of, "Okay, let me just try and get everything from my mind into your mind." Because that clearly doesn't work. You need to have it written down.

He's been pretty pleased that you've been able to build this thing, right? He's a proud father, I suspect.

I think so, yeah.

That's good. Has your mom had any influence in your development as an entrepreneur?

She's been very helpful—she's given me money to use for the company, and then said, "Just keep the money. You don't have to pay me back"— but then she also wanted me to go to college and have nothing to do with Nicko because she figured that I wouldn't be able to do both. I think her choice would have been to not do the whole BYOBiz thing and just get rid of Nicko. Do four years of college and get out and get a job, and have healthcare, retirement, a 401k.

In high school, Mom would rather I go out and spend a few hundred dollars to buy an iPod than go and buy another mower. She would never be happy if I was going out and buying a very expensive $2,000 piece of equipment to mow lawns more efficiently. She would just think I was wasting my money. And I would always say, "I could easily be going out and buying like a $300 iPod, and then 10,000 songs, but all those little bits add up. At least I'm spending my money on something that's going to make me money. An iPod, yeah, you're gonna have fun and listen to it, but the mower is gonna make probably ten times the amount."

Mom would always let me do what I wanted to do, but she would always be thinking that I was not doing what I was supposed to be doing. Instead of just going to school like everyone else, I was doing other things.

Now what about your other friends—how did they all look at what you've been doing?

Back home I have three really good friends, one of whom works with me. We've known each other since kindergarten, and we get along great. He loves Nicko because, as you can imagine, when your boss is your best friend it's the best time of your life. And my other friends love it because, even when I'm at home working, if they call

me up I have time for them, and they can come out and hang out with me. They call me Nicko. People call me that.

They're always joking around, saying, "You're gonna have this big company and I'm gonna be the head of this, and the director of that." The reality is, I have learned that you really shouldn't hire your friends because that never works out. But overall I'd say my friends think it's pretty cool, and they like it.

When you just started out, and even up through high school, you were always a little anxious about the business, because you wondered what everyone would think—but you're saying now that it turns out everybody thinks it's pretty cool.

It's funny. I think if you were to go around college saying, "Do you know Nicko? You know he owns a business and everything?" the majority of people I've met up here would say, "Yes, I know he owns a business." Whereas if you were to go to my high school and talk to the kids I've probably known since second grade, they'd probably say,

"Not really," because I'd never talk about it. It just leads into stuff like, "Ohhh, so you have a ton of money?" Unless it comes up in conversation, I never say, "Oh, I own a business," because no one likes that kid who says, "Oh, I own a business."

The cocky kid?

Yeah. Not that many people knew, whereas my friends up here love it because they can come up to the BYOBiz Center and hang out with me. And, yeah, I don't know if they love the business or if they love me. I do think I have good friends, though.

You're pretty focused on your business and your schoolwork. Do you observe that most of your compadres, although they might not have a business, have something else that they're really into?

Well, if you asked me right now to name the five most popular musicians, I wouldn't even know where to begin. Whereas other people can not only do that, but they can name the top five and then physically sing back to you the first 20 songs of each of those top five. So I feel like that's their hobby, music, and my hobby is Nicko. I don't know anything about music, but I know enough about general business, and about landscaping. I know about it and I spend my time doing it, and even when I'm not maybe doing anything, I'm definitely always thinking about it.

You mentioned that this year you have outsourced some of the operations to another contractor, which is freeing up more time for you to be more involved in school?

Exactly. The main reason why I have subcontracted out to someone else is the difficulty of providing supervision when I am so far from my work crews. You know, when the bosses aren't there to supervise, the people we were hiring weren't doing an A+ job, and it just didn't work out. And I knew that in leaving for college, leaving for Burlington, there would be zero chance I would come back to Massachusetts to write the paychecks and supervise the work.

Luckily, a kid I went to school with started a landscaping company during his sophomore year in high school, and he seemed to be doing really well. It just seemed to be the perfect match to give him my accounts, so now he's doing even better. The only thing I have to do is send the people the bills at the end of the month and answer their phone calls, and I make a percentage. I couldn't ask for anything better.

So, you're going to be out of here in three years. What are you going to do when you grow up?

Well, like I said, it's gonna be Google, General Electric, Nike, and Nicko.

Is it going to be landscaping?

No, it's going be everything. It's going to be a holding group that owns a bunch of companies. When I graduate, if I don't have the business built to a point where I can't support myself, my fail-safe plan would be to build houses. I feel like I could get a loan, and build a house for investment.

A Spec house?

Exactly, and then sell it and make some money, and then build two houses, and then three houses and four houses, and then build a development, and then maybe build a commercial building, and then build in New York, and then in Dubai. Sometimes I have dreams about that, and I think about how I'm going to build towers and everything.

But back to my ideas for Nicko. I like logistics, so I think of how it could be a logistics company. Imagine if you were a plumbing business. So, you and your friend Hank, you're plumbers, you're a business but you're not like a corporation; you're a regular plumber. The Nicko group could provide your logistics. So we'd set you up with an 800 number, a website, marketing, sales, billing and accounting, and all that. You just have to physically show up to the doorstep, do the plumbing, and then leave. And we'd send the customer a bill, and when they call your 800 number from the Yellow Pages, we'd answer it and a friendly voice would be like, "Hey, hello. What's up?" Versus the call having to go to your voicemail because you're so busy working and then you've got to bring your daughters to school and everything.

That would be a great business model with limitless growth. We can do all these tasks more efficiently than a service provider like a landscaper or plumber. Tapping into that market before everyone else does would be beneficial. So I'd want to do that. And also, I plan on helping out other people, doing charitable work. I think that would be interesting.

I really don't know where I'm going to be 10 years from now, because I want to be so many different places that I'm going have to pick one and you know, go towards it. Like I said, I have zero intentions of just graduating and going and finding a job. I plan on having a very big business.

▸▸

Nick's story illustrates very clearly the forces that an entrepreneur has to break out of in order to create and do something original. His mother, for example, is clearly torn between wanting him to do well and worrying that he might be losing his childhood and growing up too soon.

The truth is, an entrepreneur, especially a young entrepreneur, is different from most other people. He or she is not doing the same as everyone else—not family, not friends. This is one reason why it's so unusual that someone like Nick should think entrepreneurially so young. Even if you had a great idea for a business in second grade, you're simply not used to thinking and acting for yourself. You're used to doing what your friends or family are doing—which means that anyone who actually does something out of his or her own initiative seems unusual. Weird, even. The younger you start out as an entrepreneur, then, the more you're going to have to get used to being a little different from the crowd.

Nick's story also points out more clearly than any other how small a factor money is in the young entrepreneur's thinking. The principal motivation for someone to start their own business may seem to be money, but Nick's story makes it clear that he wasn't even thinking about money. And in fact, most kids don't think about money unless they really need to. They may have an allowance, they are probably used to persuading their parents to buy them things that cost more than their allowance, so money doesn't really act as a motivation to any great degree. In fact, money may become a factor in an entrepreneur's thinking only when he or she needs it for day-to-day expenses (in other words, once they get to college) or to grow the business.

It may sound very strange to say that starting a business isn't about money. In that case, what is it about? Well, another interesting aspect of Nick's story is the nature and role of entrepreneurial passion. Much has been written about the role of passion in inspiring entrepreneurs. "Follow your passion" would-be entrepreneurs are told, and this book features several young entrepreneurs whose business grew out of a personal passion. The idea that one can make a living, a good living, doing what they love or what they like to do is an extremely attractive one.

But can an entrepreneur have the same level of passion for a business that has no link to personal interest or passion? To put it another way, can the act of conceiving and building a business, whatever the nature of the business, in itself be in itself a creative act, a product of your own interest and passion?

Nick Foley claims no particular passion for cutting lawns or installing mulch, yet as you listen to Nick tell his story, you will hear him describe how, at an early age, he learned the absolute joy that can be achieved by seeing your hard work and attention to your customers help build something of value, in which you can take pride and develop true passion.

"Every week I get a message or an email thanking me...so my passion really is trying to help these people live their lives."

A LIFE IN PROGRESS Ginger Vieira

Professional Writing '08 | Hometown: Hanover, NH | Passion: Writing | Living in Progress

When you first meet Ginger Vieira, you're struck by two things—one straight away, one after a few minutes' conversation. The first is that, in a cheerful, casual way, she's one of the most powerfully-built people you've ever met. The second is that, even though she's hesitant to blow her own horn or force herself on the conversation, she is committed and determined, and when she sets her mind to something, it's going to happen. What you wouldn't guess is that she's diabetic.

Ginger has not only managed to live with chronic illness, she has managed to turn it into a strength and a purpose in life. And the same determination has helped her make the transition from being an undergraduate writing major to, a few years out of college, being an author, a diabetes counselor, a yoga instructor, a personal trainer and one of the top video bloggers in the country.

How did you first start writing about diabetes?

I first started writing for the diabetes community when I was a college sophomore. At that point I had been living with diabetes for seven or eight years. Until then, in high school and college, I had written about my life, but I'd never written about diabetes just from my own experiences. When I was in high school I was in a narrative therapy program, where they were researching to see if writing about diabetes was therapeutic for people living with diabetes, so that's probably when I first started writing about diabetes.

So is it good therapy?

Absolutely. I think it's how I cope—by writing it down. Writing it, talking about it, and supporting other people with it is how it just comes back and supports me. But most of the writing I had done in high school and college to that point was journalism, creative writing, research papers— the usual stuff you write for class.

Anyway, in my sophomore year I wrote a personal essay about how I still went to see my pediatrician about my diabetes rather than a specialist because pediatricians are much better at dealing with patients as people. I sent it to an online health advice company called HealthCentral, and they published it. In fact, they liked it so much they hired me to write a blog for them every week about living with diabetes.

At first the blog was very unstructured—it was just me writing. I continued writing for them over the course of two years, at which point it evolved into a new website called DiabeTeens that they designed specifically for teens with diabetes. They made me the main figurehead of that website, so it was no longer freelance writing, it was salaried writing, which was a nice way to get through college!

How did you get into weightlifting, and how did that play into your career?

During the time I was working for HealthCentral, after I graduated, I was also beginning to compete in powerlifting. I had joined a gym and learned how to weight-lift more. I'd gotten really strong over the course of a year working with a trainer. The whole reason I joined the gym was because I wanted to learn more about how to take care of myself. I had no major intentions of competing. Somebody saw me bench pressing with my trainer and said, "Jeez, you oughta get that girl in a powerlifting competition." We had no idea what competitive numbers were for my body size, so this other guy gave us a training program and helped us learn the basics and the rules.

Six months later, in my first competition, I ended up setting seven records within that federation in my weight class. I set my record with a 175-pound bench press, a 300-pound dead lift and a 265-pound squat.

When I set those records I blogged about it for HealthCentral, and that made me stand out in this vague thing called the "diabetes online community." Four or five years ago, there were a number of diabetes blogs and online communities and support groups, and people were getting to know each other. Today that has evolved massively into what's called the DOC, the Diabetes Online Community. There are about 35 names in the DOC that are known for diabetes

advocacy, and I'm known within that group of 35 for fitness and video blogging. So the powerlifting really helped me to establish my niche within the diabetes community.

How did you go from writing about diabetes into health coaching?

When I first started the weightlifting I also started falling in love with being in the gym all the time. That year, my senior year at college, I was also getting certified in being an Ashtanga Yoga instructor. That's a 200-hour course spread out over a year. And then I did my certification to be a personal trainer.

That all came along before the idea of being a health coach. So for three years, right after college, I worked for that gym as a yoga instructor and personal trainer. Finally I realized that what I love doing is supporting people and helping them make progress, mostly around their health, but also in the way that they think about themselves.

So then one of my personal training clients said,

"Hey, check out this program." It was the David Rock coaching program. It's called Results Coaching. It's usually geared toward corporate coaching, but I really liked the method and the science and how it was using brain-based studies, so I geared it toward diabetes and health coaching.

It was a six month program but it started face-to-face for a weekend and ended face-to-face for a weekend, and in between it consisted of online courses over a span of six months. I took that program at the same time as I was working as a personal trainer, and then at the end of that, I started establishing my business.

So today your business is...

Today my business is Living in Progress, and it's health and diabetes coaching. I'm trained in a cognitive-focused coaching method where you're helping people look at the way they think, and how the way they think is impacting the way they take care of themselves.

How many customers do you have?

The most clients I had at one time was eight. Then for a while I took a job with a major diabetes organization, which basically made my own business flatten out. When I finished up that job I had five different clients. Now that I'm able to focus more on my own business, I'm building my clientele and expanding my work with other diabetes-focused coaching programs, as well as more motivational speaking.

And all the coaching you do, is that face-to-face or online?

It's usually over the phone.

So if I have celiac disease—I do have celiac disease—I might find you and say hey, I'm having trouble coping with this thing, and you'd say, okay, let's work together, I can help you.

I do have some clients from the Burlington area, but it's mostly online. I'm very flexible with what I set up because everyone has different needs. Some people really want me to coach them in exercise and write programs for them, and because I have diabetes they like coming to me more than they like going to some random person in their gym who's a trainer. And for some people it's a really emotional struggle that they have to work through, so that's when we meet once a week on the phone for an hour, and that's where I can really apply the coaching methods that I'd used.

With diabetes, the day-to-day coping is the hardest part. Even if you're taking your insulin and checking your blood sugar, the disease is 24/7, nonstop. I don't know what I would do with all of the energy that I use thinking about diabetes if I didn't have diabetes to take up all that energy. I don't have trouble coping with it—diabetes seems to empower me more than anything else—but it takes up so much energy in your head all day long. To control your blood sugar is one of the hardest things to do. It's such a common thing for a non-diabetic to say, "Oh, as long as you control your blood sugar, you're fine, right?" But I spend a lot of my energy all day trying to control my blood sugar because there are so many variables. My body doesn't make

any insulin, right? I have Type 1 diabetes. (Type 2 you still make insulin but you don't make enough to support your body's needs.) A normal body makes insulin, drip-drip-drip all day long, and if I gain weight or lose weight, if I stop exercising or I start exercising I'm going to need more or less insulin. And as a diabetic I have to adjust it myself. People can't really understand what it's like unless they're going through it.

And you can't really advise someone on dosages, you can just advise them on how to cope with the fact that they're going to have this process ongoing in their life.

I'm not a doctor. I don't tell people what insulin to take. I do help people learn how things like exercise impact their blood sugar, and then help them think through their own knowledge of what they already know about their diabetes so they can say, "Oh, maybe I'll adjust my insulin this way."

Another thing I help people do on the cognitive side, though, is help them change the way they view their diabetes. It's really common to resent it and be really pissed off and wonder why you have to deal with all this shit every day, and all that resentment and anger really stops them from taking care of themselves. You're the only person who can really take care of your diabetes every day, so if you decide to skip your insulin it's going to impact your health in a big way. So part of the blogging, my mission, is to encourage people to see their diabetes as a challenge in their life.

We all have challenges, whether or not you have a disease. When I was diagnosed I went through the list of all my friends and was like, "She's got leukemia, he has two parents who are alcoholic...." I literally listed off all my friends in the seventh grade and realized that everyone's got something. Diabetes is just one of my somethings.

The coaching methods I've learned really apply to anything. It's about learning how to have a conversation where I'm no longer giving advice or telling you what I think, I'm helping you understand yourself better. You come up with your own answers, but I'm helping to guide you through that.

How did you make yourself into a multi-media diabetes celebrity?

One of the most important things in my work with diabetes is networking. I've gotten a lot of opportunities through Twitter, LinkedIn, and Facebook. I hated Twitter when they first started it. I thought it was so dumb, but I felt obligated to use it because the diabetes community is there, and I've gotten radio interviews because of that, I've gotten published, written interviews. My last job I basically got because I found the CEO on LinkedIn and got his email from LinkedIn and sent him a release when my book came out and he saw my video blogs. So social media have become an expertise of mine, in addition to my name and building my place within the DOC. I have about 3,000 diabetic friends on Facebook, and that's the main area where I advertised my book. I can post something about diabetes and exercise, what I did that day, or I can post my blood sugar, and within the day sometimes there'll be 50, 60 likes or sometimes 30 comments within just a few hours because that's where I share my diabetic life.

When I established my business last year I really looked at Facebook differently. I consciously sought out people who were diabetic, and when they accepted a friend request from me I would take the time to go to their page and say "Hey, I'm Ginger. I've lived with Type 1 for thirteen years. This is my website. Here are some video blogs I've made." I posted that on their page and it just started kind of exploding from there.

The video blogs are funny things that just evolved. I love doing them. My first few were a little bumpy, but now I really know how to make them look clean. I just use my laptop and I kneel on the floor with a blank backdrop behind me and I put a lamp in my face so it looks well lit. It's usually taking a topic and talking about it for three minutes, in a way that's not just me talking. I've learned over the course of a year how to make them entertaining, how to edit with iMovie so it's not just one long clip. Sometimes I pull words onto the screen—I've gotten better at making it entertaining. I post them on my YouTube channel,

and I've built a following because of it.

I've started doing a lot more public speaking because of the video blogs I've made, and I'm hoping to do more. The presentation I'm doing in Utah next week I got asked to do because of a video blog I made slam-poetry style. Then I made one about why I love the people in the DOC, and so somebody suggested to a hospital that hosts a diabetes mixer—it's a big event they have every year (they're having two this year because it's become so successful). They asked if I would come and perform diabetes slam poetry, and I said, "Sure! Do you want me to host the whole thing?" So now they're flying me out there to host the whole event.

How do you see your future from a career standpoint?

Well, you know, I'm still trying, and I hate that I'm still trying to figure it out because I always want to be five years ahead of everyone else. But I'm not. I'm just 25. I need to just slow down.

I recently gave 30–40 hours of my week to a company that hired me to sit in front of a computer and talk about diabetes, and it made me realize I don't want to be sitting in front of a computer all the time, I want to be able to exercise with people in real life and teach yoga.

The biggest hurdle for me in my business is money to market and money to advertise. I don't have the funding to spend, so I'm teaming up with a couple of websites who I really believe in and who appreciate what I do. I'll be teaching online courses that I've designed for people who have diabetes. I know David Edelman, who founded *Diabetes Daily* and has just started Diabetes University. When I went to work for this other company he said, "All right, I'll see you on the other side." Now it's the other side and I said, "All right David, here I am."

Tell me about your diabetes book.

I wrote this whole book, *Your Diabetes Science Experiment*, based on my own research in trying to be a powerlifter with diabetes. The book is not about powerlifting, it's about human physiology, but when I first started powerlifting I told my doctor and he rolled his eyes at me. I was so pissed that he wasn't going to support me and didn't believe in it that I decided to prove him wrong and write the book about it.

I wrote it between about March and September 2010. Two young women, Jillian Towne and Emma Crockett, did the editing, John Brown did all of the layout and design—they're all Champlain undergraduates—and my friend Ashley, who is a Champlain alum, did the photography. They were awesome and efficient. John Brown really had the biggest job. He constantly had to come up with page templates, and was very flexible. He'd show me something and I'd say, "Oh, I don't really like that," and he'd say, "Okay, I'll find something better." There was never any debate or argument, he just worked with me.

We printed it through Lulu.com, and the book came out in January 2011.

What advice would you give young people thinking about starting their own business?

First of all, you need to cultivate what you love

doing the most. When I'm doing a video blog, for example, I don't really get paid for those, but that doesn't really feel like work to me. And it's promoting my business. So, cultivate what you really love doing and then figure out how that serves other people. That's the first step. And then, as my dad always reminds me, hire people to do the things that you're not good at doing. That's something that I haven't done enough of yet, because financially I'm not in the position to do that, but I need to do it more.

What would you say is your passion?

My passion? What drives me the most? Every week I get a message or an email thanking me for making a particular video because it made them cry or it made them laugh, so my passion really is trying to help these people live their lives. Writing is one way that I serve that purpose, but it's the people that I care about the most.

I made one video blog—which became really popular really quickly—using duct tape. There's this debate about the fact that insulin is not a cure, it's a treatment: people say diabetics are fine, they have insulin, but it doesn't fix us, it's just a way of helping us live longer. So I did this funny thing where I went around my house and tore things in half and duct taped them back together and said, "See, it kind of works but it's not perfect. Duct tape doesn't last forever; neither does insulin." I almost didn't put it up because I thought it was so dumb, but people loved it—because I was being silly, but I was making a really serious point at the same time. That's what I try to do with every video. Things I make really can make an impact.

▸▸

The development path of Ginger's business is typical of many entrepreneurs in that it is not linear. Ginger did not start by writing a business plan that laid out five years' worth of strategies, actions, and financial projections. Ginger just waded in, and as she got active in the marketplace and grew familiar with the lay of the land, opportunities came her way, and she had the presence of mind to recognize them as opportunities, seize them and make them happen. Her guiding light was her passion for writing and the realization that she wanted to make a difference for diabetics and others with chronic diseases.

This is true not only in a general sense, but in the specifics. When she wrote her first diabetes column she didn't know anything about Twitter or social marketing. She picked up what she needed along the way. She even worked out how to be a successful and charismatic video blogger by using equipment that was already in her own living room.

It's also interesting to me that if, before this had all happened, Ginger had announced, "I am going to create a successful business by writing about coping with diabetes," who would have thought her a serious entrepreneur? No one. Yet Ginger's personal drive and vision were so strong that it is becoming a reality, and I suspect that millions of people will profoundly benefit before she is through.

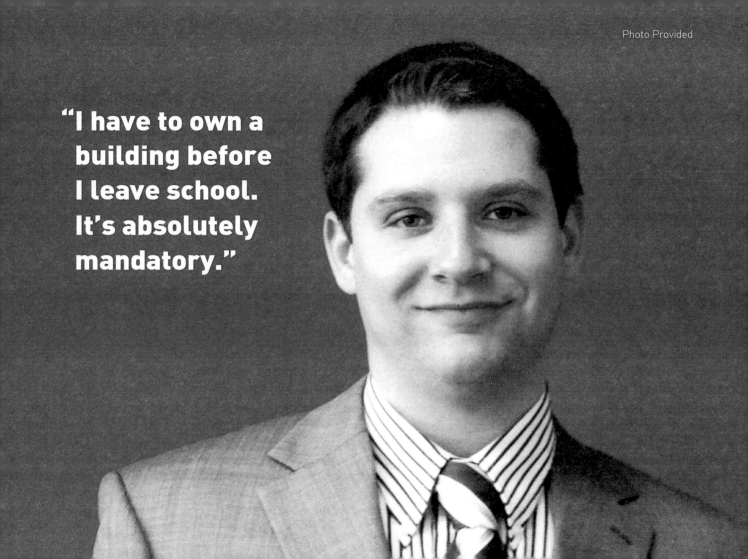

"I have to own a
building before
I leave school.
It's absolutely
mandatory."

FUTURE REAL ESTATE MOGUL Alex Wolff

Business '13 | Hometown: McLean, VA | Passion: Real Estate Investment

I met Alex early in his freshman year. He was a very serious young man, and he kept trying to focus our first conversation on whether his participation in the BYOBiz program meant that he could "get a loan from BYOBiz to buy some property." I had to break it to him that BYOBiz couldn't actually lend him a couple of million to buy a few buildings, but I admired his nerve—and his ambition! At the same time, I couldn't help noticing that he talked down into his chest, and it was easy to see he wasn't as confident as he sounded.

Two years later, Alex's demeanor is only slightly less serious but he remains as focused as ever. He projects a wonderful self-confidence now—still quiet, but self-confident—and you get the sense he is listening to everything very carefully.

When you were a kid, when did you first think about entrepreneurship or maybe having your own business?

This will probably sound pretty stupid, but I was watching *The Thomas Crown Affair*, where Pierce Brosnan's an art thief who runs this big company that does mergers and acquisitions. I was really into skateboarding at the time, but something about the movie made me think that business might be a way to go—though I had no idea what kind of business or even if it was possible. I just thought that it would be pretty cool and I would want to do something like that.

How old were you at the time and what else was going on in your life, other than skateboarding?

Probably 13 at that time. Before I got any interest in business, I just lived and breathed skateboarding all day, every day. Then as I got a little more into business, I leaned away from that.

What did you like in school?

I'd say I liked English a little bit, and history, but hated math and science. I couldn't understand it at all.

So you started with this little inspiration with *The Thomas Crown Affair*, Pierce Brosnan—good looking guy, you related well to that—so how did it go from there? How did your development as an entrepreneur and your curiosity about entrepreneurship or business grow?

Well, I didn't really do anything for maybe a year or two, but it made me think suits were cool! Then when I was 14 years old I read *Rich Dad, Poor Dad* by Robert Kiyosaki, and that book dramatically changed the course of my life forever. After reading it, I felt that there was no possible way that I could let myself get a job and go to work for someone else. I said to myself, "That's crazy. I'll never do that. I just have to start some kind of business and invest in something."

Who put you onto that book?

I found it in my parents' office, and it just looked good, so I thought I'd read it. It explained assets and wealth creation in such simple, blatant, hit-you-over-the-head terms that it really spoke to me, grabbed me, and I read the whole thing right there.

Were either of your parents involved in business in a way that influenced you—other than leaving the book where you could find it?

My mom is an executive with the SRA. She does project management stuff and works on a lot of government contracts, so she's always been involved in business—but not in the way that I am. I definitely admired her work ethic, with hours that were just grueling, having to bring your work home with you a lot, and being constantly tied to your Blackberry. I knew that I'd probably be getting into something like that, but I wasn't sure I'd be able to handle the lifestyle. Taking calls if you're out on vacation, or not going on vacation because you needed to do certain stuff with work. It seemed like a very big undertaking, and 80 percent of the game was just showing up. I could definitely see her doing

that every single day, and it showed me that if you really want to do something, the first part is just being there all the time.

Does anything from high school comes to mind as being formative or influential for you?

I didn't have a lot of guidance in high school. I knew I wanted to do something with business. I got an account with E*TRADE, the online international brokerage company, in 2007. My account lost about 70 percent of its value in the first couple months.

Did you beat the market, though?

No, no. I didn't do very well. I don't think the market had anything to do with it—it was mostly just my stock picks. But I did the e-trading, and I got interested in flipping houses and assigning contracts, and thought that was really cool. From what I had read in a bunch of Robert Kiyosaki books—the ones that come after *Rich Dad, Poor Dad*—it seemed like a good way to get into the real estate market, and actually form an LLC. I thought that meant you were really doing something—and then I realized that it was just filing paperwork and it doesn't really make your business go forward. So that went away. I was basically just planning and deciding what I wanted to do and how it would relate to college.

So Kiyosaki was more of an influence than just that first book; he steered you toward real estate as an area where you could do what he was suggesting in his first book?

Well, he just laid out investing as a world with all these different vehicles. I thought stocks were kind of risky and I didn't exactly know how to build a business or what product I would sell. Most millionaires in America made it off of real estate. At the time I was really money-driven but didn't know exactly what I wanted to do, so I thought real estate was a good way to get into it. I figured out that I liked it a little, but reading a lot more of Kiyosaki's books, like *Rich Dad's Guide to Investing: What the Rich Invest in, That the Poor and the Middle Class Do Not* and *Rich Dad's Cashflow Quadrant: Rich Dad's Guide to Financial Freedom*, it really just put real estate investing as the most obvious, logical, best kind of business for me to build.

What was the connection you made with real estate? What made it seem good for you?

The mechanics of the deal were what drew me to it. I didn't really think that a house itself was that cool—it was the way to finance something and get really creative so you could buy something you couldn't afford. It seemed like the mechanics of the deals could be engineered to become something like a mad scientist.

Were there any other sources or resources you used to broaden your learning in this area? Any people?

I read other stuff online, but I'd say that in high school, most of that all came from Kiyosaki.

You mentioned that you were thinking about college during all of this. So could you say that your interest in this was a

prime driver for college?

I didn't really think about college too much. My options were a little limited because of my academics; I had a low grade point average throughout high school and generally did not like conventional schooling. I was also in a special education program due to suffering from ADHD. But I got a college counselor and said I wanted to start a business the day after orientation, and that I wanted the college to pay for it and help me do it—in other words, give me advisers and all kinds of people to show me the way—and he looked into that for a while. It came down to Champlain in Vermont and some college near Lake Tahoe. After evaluating them, I said, "Bring Your Own Business? All right. Sounds good." Tahoe was a little far away and I didn't know too much about Vermont, but the BYOBiz program sounded like exactly what I wanted.

So you get to college and obviously we've been working together. So, how do you see your last two years? What progress have you made?

I've definitely gotten direction and a lot of experience, and I can say I pretty much know the steps going forward from this point, which is a lot more than I had when I got here. Through BYOBiz, I have made several amazing connections (so far), and that's where it all started. In the first year, I was talking to you, and I was trying to decide what I wanted to do and I kind of floundered. I didn't really do too much with it, but after you introduced me to a guy in the area named Scott Rieley, a major real estate developer in the community, things started to happen. I started working with him every week and he assumed a mentor role with me and helped me learn the business of real estate investment and management.

Scott Rieley has been my real estate investment mentor for about a year and a half now. We discuss how to buy and manage real estate investments as well as general business advice. Scott shares how he got to where he is today, which is inspiring to me. I am currently searching for my first property to buy, and Scott will be my principal investor.

The second really good connection I made was with Adam Hergenrother. I remember you called me up and said, "I have someone here that you should meet. Just get down here right now," on a Saturday morning early, and I said, "This has got be good." It was.

I came down to your office, met Adam, and I remember Adam said, "I'll tell you what I've done with my business and my life in three minutes." My jaw basically dropped to the ground. Adam was still in his twenties and he was flying high. After graduating from college, he had set up his own real estate sales company, a branch of international real estate agency Keller Williams. Adam's getting national recognition. So I started working for him as an intern at Keller Williams Realty Green Mountain Properties, his own real estate firm, here in Vermont.

I interned there for a while, figuring out what he was doing, but eventually I had maxed out the learning as an intern so Adam suggested I get my real estate license. Right away. I took the test in May 2011, on my 20th birthday, and passed it. It was a bear—lots to study and memorize while still doing my classwork. But I am so happy I did it, it's been amazing and a lot of fun. Working at Keller Williams as a buyer specialist, I've already closed one deal and have another under contract, and I have a couple clients I'm working with. I'm just learning how business is done and how to interact with people. And that's the best.

And while I am doing sales for Keller Wiliams, I have my eye out for investment properties that I can buy for my own account. I have a couple of people, including my mentors, committed to investing with me if I find the right property.

I remember your struggle learning about networking. Can you talk about that experience?

I'd say networking has just been my biggest tool. I think it should be anybody's biggest tool if you're an entrepreneur—or with anything you want to do. All the books, all the blogs, have said to talk to people who are doing what you want to do, people who are successful. Get out there and find out what they're doing.

Just by being a college student, if you just reach

out to someone, there's no downside. People will have you come and talk to them, they'll tell you how they did it. They'll lead you. People love talking about themselves, and they'll help you a lot if you just reach out to them. It might be something that you might not ever think to do, but it's so vital to any success in anything you want to do in this area. You need a guy who has done it before to tell you what to do. You won't do everything perfectly through networking, but it will help you make a lot fewer mistakes and really set you on a much better path if you know what you're doing by talking to people.

I remember you networking with Jack DuBrul [a larger-than-life entrepreneur in Vermont, the owner of Automaster and other automobile dealerships and ventures]. How hard was it to make that first contact with him?

Well, it wasn't too much of a struggle to actually make the connection. I think the struggle was being a 19-year-old college student and trying—in an hour-long meeting—to make a good connection with a big business person in the community who has a big personality, and trying to make that connection work. Through my real estate career, it's gotten a lot easier, but before, just going out and talking to Jack—he was a big, intimidating guy and I expected him to say, "Oh, Alex, you're in college? Oh, that's so cool. Here's what I did. I'll help you out," but he kind of stood there with his arms crossed and just said, "What do you want?" and he pushed me into the deep end of the pool. It really forces you to articulate your thoughts and to try to have a good adult conversation about business.

We met and it was great. He gave me an Automaster hat. He told me to go out and read *Atlas Shrugged*, by Ayn Rand. I said no problem. Now, that's 1,300 pages. So I'm still in the process of reading that, about four or five hundred pages in, but I absolutely will go back and talk to him soon.

When you look back on your first two years at college, do you see anything in the classroom that's been particularly

useful or meaningful to you?

The availability of my professors to talk through my issues in my business. The small classes. Being able to have interactions with teachers without anything to lose. Getting to have these conversations with people about business.

I think one thing we don't realize as college students is that we sound a lot different than adults sometimes. I think etiquette and learning how to handle yourself has been the biggest thing for me. When I'm sitting in a real estate meeting for the firm where I work, some people think that I'm thirty. I attribute that to close conversations that I've had with a lot of professors about business and about real estate. That's given me a no-risk safe zone to practice having these conversations that I'm not used to having with kids in a dorm room.

Do you think many of your student peers are doing anything like what you're doing—whatever their interests are?

Absolutely. I don't know what it is—maybe it's Vermont, maybe it's Burlington, maybe it's

Champlain or the University of Vermont, but I definitely see a lot of entrepreneurial spirit on campus and around town. It seems like the area is a small incubator for ideas. So many people open up a storefront or start a snowboarding company—there's so many different ideas and so many different people who are producing them.

You've got two more years in school. How do you see your future rolling out?

I'm not sure. I'm working with Scott to buy buildings. I have to own a building before I leave school. It's absolutely mandatory.

I really want to explore the real estate agent career a little bit. One thing that sounds exciting right now is that there are only a few real estate agents in your community—whichever that is—who really make a lot of money and are really the biggest producers. You'll find that only five percent of agents do about 80 percent of the deals in the community. Once you reach that level, you only need to maintain that for a year or two and then you have a lot of significant pull to start your own firm, to go overseas, to some other place. For me, achieving that level of celebrity and accomplishment at least as a real estate agent is probably going to be the next big step. I don't want to be a real estate agent forever or even be a mega-producing real estate agent for 10 years. I definitely want to start my own company specializing in real estate sales or investing. Developing and managing both really interest me.

The short-term goal of a career in real estate sales is just a credential so that you can then go out and attract capital? So not only the knowledge you've gained, but your credentials say that you're a player in the real estate business, that people should take you seriously as you start putting together your own deals?

Yeah, I realized that right now I don't have any particular value to anybody. You need to create value in order to become or to have your business become influential. Right now as a college student, I'm just a real estate agent. That only means I have a license. You really need to prove to people that you're able to bring real value and that your brain is actually worth money, that your ideas are going to produce results. Being that kind of big producer as a real estate agent really opens the door to so many other business opportunities. It puts you on such a different level with different players that it sets you up for success in almost any other thing that you want.

So you're 20 years old, and you've accomplished a lot more than I did when I was twenty. Any words of advice for those who may come after you?

Just do it. Who cares if your idea isn't perfect, or if it's not tweaked? Tell some people about it, get some feedback, and go do it. If not, it's only going to be an idea. That's the biggest thing that stops people—they don't want to get deterred, they don't want to look stupid, or they don't want to make mistakes. Forget about all that. None of that matters. It doesn't matter what people think of you—just go do it. Start as soon as you can. If it's something you actually care about, it'll make you happy. And if you care about it, work hard. It's an amazing feeling to get out there and start doing it. No one's going to do it for you, so you need to take that initiative as soon as possible. Get off the couch, and go do it.

What does your mom think?

She thinks it's pretty cool. In the beginning, it was amused skepticism, and now she thinks it's going pretty well. She hears what I'm doing with Scott and Adam. She's thinking maybe she'll send me up some money to invest for them, and I obviously have to think about that, but it's nice that even if they're your parents, there's some recognition, and even if it's just one person, somebody knows that you're doing something right. That's good. So yeah, she's excited for what's going to happen, and I'm sure probably a little nervous.

Now what do your friends think about it all?

This thing is weird with friends. When you're doing something that's so ahead of what many other people are doing, they don't like it. They don't want to see you be successful. It makes them uncomfortable. Even if they're very smart and talented themselves, it's like how everybody still hates the Yankees.

For instance, if all your friends are landscapers and you come talking about this big deal you just put together, no one wants to hear that. A lot of my good friends are happy for me and excited to see me succeed, but you'll definitely find friends who don't totally care about your commitment or maybe aren't happy about what they're doing, they'll fall to the wayside because success freaks people out. Some people don't want to see you doing well—they want to see you stay at their level. That's one of the main things I didn't think of or have any idea about going into this. It was a big surprise to me, but it's definitely something to think about. It'll happen.

But you've made your peace with that.

Yeah. It's just something you have to deal with. Deep down, what I want to do is build a company, and that's at the forefront of my thoughts right now. That's what matters the most. And the people who don't want to see you succeed? You shouldn't be friends with them anyway. Eventually, if once you start doing really well and people can see that, you'll get due recognition.

We've talked a little about networking, and you've put key people in your network. When you think about your network going forward? Are there any people or kinds of people in certain positions that you want to get connected with?

Anybody who's smarter than me. Anybody that's done something like what I'm doing. People who are successful in any field are really helpful. In my business, members of the community who are substantial, people who know the area. I'm trying to invest in Shelburne. Maybe somebody who's lived there—even a farmer who's lived in Shelburne for 30 years has something to tell me, can give me something I can understand. If Vermont isn't where I decide to stay, which is possible, I'll find the town I want to go live in and

chase down the biggest investors and business owners, the people who the buzz is about. They're easy to find. Those are the people you want to get to know. I'll seek them out and buy them lunch. And if they say no the first time, I'll call them again. And again.

▸▸

It's fascinating to me that Alex pinpoints his picking up that Kiyosaki book from his parents' desk and reading it as a critical turning point in his life. How remarkable that what was arguably a trivial moment turned out to be so important to Alex's life. What caused him to do that? Curiosity? What was it about that book title, or the cover design, that caused him to pick it up? Maybe he was just ready at that point in his life to take in the message of that book?

What any young entrepreneur can take from Alex's story is how ready Alex is to try things that he feels in some way may be important to him. I know it was tough for him to contact Jack DuBrul. I must have looked at six or more versions of the original letter he drafted to Jack, but Alex wouldn't let go. No matter how hard it was to write the letter, he was going to have that meeting. No matter how hard it was to cram for that real estate licensing exam on short notice, he was determined to do it.

I also want to point out that Alex's early passion for skateboarding, which some might see as a sign that he was a rebel or he was irresponsible, was a sign that he was able to throw himself wholeheartedly into something that mattered to him. Many of these young entrepreneurs started out by being really into sports of some kind; in their case it was a sign that they had a drive and a passion that over time could be transferred into something completely different—starting and running a business, for example.

Along the same lines, it's interesting that Alex hated math and science in school, and as he says, he couldn't understand it at all. That's not necessarily a sign that someone hasn't got "a head for numbers," and won't be able to handle business. It may be a sign that, as in Alex's case, he just hadn't yet found a good enough reason to want to learn math. Starting your own business may be the best reason of all!

One other point: it may seem to you that if you don't have a parent who is a businessperson who can teach you all about business you'll be at a big disadvantage, or maybe that the whole subject is so complicated you'll never be able to make a go of it on your own. In Alex's case, though, what he learned from his mother was something that may be deeper and stronger—a work ethic. Watching her, he knew how hard he'd have to push, what hours he'd have to put in, and it didn't scare him. Having a good work ethic is much more likely to mean you'll learn about business than if your family is in business but your own work ethic is, well, lacking.

It doesn't take much time with Alex to know that Alex is going to go where Alex wants to go–and nothing is going to stop him.

"I liked the fact that it was my own blood, sweat, and tears that was making that money."

FINE TUNING Paxton Hall

International Business '14 | Hometown: Victor, NY | Passion: Creating & Building Businesses | PaxTunz

Paxton Hall is one of those people who got the entrepreneurial bug early—at the age of seven, to be exact. Unlike some of the others in this book who had a particular passion in life and found that entrepreneurship is a great vehicle to help them build a life around that passion, Paxton found his passion was growing and building the business itself—and that passion translates to almost any business. In telling the story of his entrepreneurial journey (so far), Pax touches on the many ways owning and building your own business can be deeply satisfying.

If you can think back in your life, when was that first inkling that you were interested in things that maybe later you found out would be called entrepreneurial ventures?

When I was younger, we lived on the back of a golf course in Rochester, New York. My parents would go on runs on the golf course and they would always find a bunch of stray balls. After a few years—I was seven or eight at the time—they amassed two garbage cans full of golf balls, and they said, "You know what, Paxton? This summer, you should go on the side of the golf course. We'll set you up a little cart full of the golf balls. We'll clean the golf balls and you should sell golf balls and lemonade."

Being seven or eight and wanting to prove to my parents that I could do it, I was like, "Yeah! Why not? I'll make a bunch of money. Go buy more Power Rangers!"

The deal was three golf balls and a glass of lemonade for a dollar. I would sit there for eight, nine hours a day. In the first two years, I'd be lucky to make maybe $5 a day, but after a few years it really started to pick up. I got a lot of repeat customers and people started to know me. They're like, "That kid on the eleventh hole on South Course? He's selling good balls." By the time I was about 10 I started to really rake in the money. I was making about $1000 a summer as a 10-year-old.

Really?

Yeah. We'd spiced it up a little bit when I'd learned Pro V1 and NikeOne and Callaways were better balls. I had a different deal for them: you could get two of those balls and a glass of lemonade for $1.50. That would definitely be my first brush with entrepreneurship.

It was funny, because this one guy in particular, Mike Stevens, he would always come by and he was like, "How's my little entrepreneur doing? He's saving up for his college fund?" and I was like, "Am I really an entrepreneur? Is that what this is?" Looking back, that's exactly what it was, and it makes perfect sense that I've fallen into this way of life.

What was it about all that that kept you going, or kept you interested?

It was just so much fun, for several reasons. I mean, hey, I was 10, I was making way more money than any of my friends with their allowances, but it was also, I got to know a lot of people and I got to have these relationships with these adults that I normally wouldn't have any exposure to. And I got to sell. I learned how to haggle a little bit.

One time in particular when I was 11, this guy came by and said, "I'll take your whole cart for $50." I was like, "Fifty dollars? Are you kidding me? There's like three hundred balls here," so I actually got him up to $150 and he still took the whole cart. I liked all of it, and I liked the fact that it was my own blood, sweat and tears that was making that money.

How long did you run that?

I ran that until I was, I think, fourteen. The biggest summer I ever had was $2,300, when I was twelve. At 14, I handed it off to my little brother Kameron, who's now 15, and he later handed it off to our youngest brother Hayden, who's still doing it every summer. So it's kind of a family business.

Oh, man! So you're 14 years old; did you sell the business or just hand it off?

I handed it off. I think I was getting a little too old, and part of the appeal was, "Oh, there's this young little kid..."

I gotcha. What was your next adventure?

The next adventure wasn't until junior year of high school. The Kauffman Foundation had donated a bunch of funds to the University of Rochester and they started a program called The Young Entrepreneurs Academy. I thought, I'm taking a bunch of business classes—why not give it a shot? It was free through the high school, so I signed up.

I had this idea for a ski/snowboard boot backpack. I'd been on a ski team for four years at this point, and I'd seen the horrors of all the different ways people tried to deal with their ski boots—over the shoulder, attached to a backpack, in really big, bulky backpacks—so I did the Academy program and designed this little backpack. Unfortunately for me, the economic recession hit right about the same time this program was going on, so most of the funding for my high school's program got pulled. So that ended up being a half-baked idea.

So you come to college, and what have you been doing now?

Last winter I was talking to Tom Myers, an International Businesses professor here, and he was trying to get me to start a ski team. Unfortunately, the timing of that didn't really pan out too well, so we abandoned it. But he had given me this idea: "Hey, you should just do a tune-up shop on campus."

I went home for Christmas break and while sitting on this tune-up shop idea, I thought, "Well, there are really only two places in Burlington where you can get your skis or snowboards tuned up: Ski Rack, downtown on Main Street, or The Alpine Shop, up on Dorset Street. So college kids are in a jam if they can't tune their own skis and

boards." At that point I figured, "You know what? I just need to do it—just give it a shot. If it doesn't work, it doesn't work, but if it works, then there's definitely something there."

At the point where I really committed, I was on this website, ArtechSki.com, ordering all the supplies, and it ended up being $400 for all the vices, the wax, the files, the stones and all that. Luckily, I hooked up with Noah Goldblatt, who is the senior advisor at the Study Abroad office. He had connections that helped me get 15 percent off the equipment plus free snowboard vises, so that sweetened the deal. But once I clicked that Purchase button, I was completely committed to it.

Since then I've opened this ski and snowboard tune-up shop on campus. It's called PaxTunz and now it's actually going to be a bike tune-up shop too, through the help of a new freshman. Last year I made about $200 over the break-even point, so it was pretty successful and it was a lot of fun.

And you only started operating at the end of the season, as I recall.

I opened it kind of in the middle of February, through the beginning of April. It was very hard because it was mid-season and I had no recognition. This year I've already got a whole bunch of people who were like, "Oh, yeah! I heard about you last year but I didn't really know your hours and that kind of stuff so I never brought it in. This year I'm totally going to bring it to you." I'm going to get way ahead of the game and it should be a lot better.

Interesting. What do you think it is about you that makes you gravitate to this kind of stuff?

I would say I like being in control. I don't like being in groups at school; I always end up doing all the work. The other thing is, I just like taking initiative, I like getting things done, I like starting things, I like creating things. That's a lot of fun to me. I would also say just creating things and seeing them succeed also gives me a lot of satisfaction too. I'm the kind of person who's like,

"This is a great idea. We should run with it."

If you think about PaxTunz: you had this idea, and you said, "By gosh, I'm going to do it." What did you do first?

The first thing I did was talk to the staff here at Champlain to find a space to do it. I started talking to Michel George, who is the VP of Planning and Facilities, about finding a space to do this and I started talking to Lisa Mazzariello, who's the director of the Student Life Center because I figured I'd probably do it in that building.

Because of student traffic?

Correct. That was actually my biggest hurdle. Finding a space hung me up the longest because everybody was worried about setting off fire alarms and me making a mess—rightly so, because there are a few people I know who, if they had done this idea, would have completely left it a mess, and they probably could have set off the fire alarm! In the end, I realized I needed to just set up shop and do it one night and prove to them that I wasn't going to make a huge mess and business was going to be successful and good for the community of the college.

What's interesting to me is that you did some planning, but not a lot of planning.

I didn't do a ton of planning. I talked to a lot of different students and faculty to see if this was a worthy idea. I did a good bit of financial planning, seeing, "Okay, this is the rough estimate of what I need to start this." Then, doing some forecasting to see how many customers or how many skis and boards, what I need to break even and to start making some money.

Beforehand I put up some posters around campus, I sent a lot of emails, I talked to a few staff and as many students as I could. I just tried to get the word out. I made a Facebook group and I sent out an APB on the social media.

The first night I think I got five or six customers, so the first night was pretty successful and it was a good measurement of what was to come. That being said, there were a lot of nights where I wouldn't get anybody and I'd just be sitting there,

tuning my own skis and just talking to people. There was never a night when I didn't talk to a prospective customer; I always got at least a few people who came by and were like, "Oh, this is where you are! I don't have my board or skis with me but now I know where you are, and I know your hours, I'm going to bring them to you."

By the end of the season I was starting to get more name recognition and people knew where I was and there was definitely a few, two or three weeks there, where I would get a whole bunch of equipment at about eight or nine o'clock and I'd be tuning until about two in the morning and be bringing stuff to peoples' dorms then.

What are your plans for this season? I know you said you were really going to crank it up. What are you thinking specifically?

I'm working with a freshman student and we're going to turn it into a bike shop as well. I don't have a website, so I'm working with a senior marketing student on that and we're really going to batten down the hatches as far as social media and marketing goes, because that was definitely my weakest point. I have a friend at the University of Vermont and I have a friend at St. Michael's College; I'm going to try to coordinate with them to do something similar there and see if it works on other college campuses.

Are you going to offer some kind of early pre-season special to get some volume in before the snow flies or anything like that?

Yeah, I'd say I'm probably going to do a 20 percent discount and then I'm also going to have punch cards so if you get two or three tunes, you get one free, or you get one half price. And a referral thing: if you bring a friend with you or a friend comes in, "Oh, so-and-so told me to come here," then you get 50 percent off.

If this thing goes this year, you've got three more years of school—you figure you'll just run it and then hand it off to someone else?

I think the dream goal is to have somebody in the investment world see it and be like, "You know what? This would be a cool thing to franchise at other college campuses, especially out West and at other places in Vermont." But realistically speaking, (and I think it would need to involve a name change) I see handing off to somebody at the end of my four years. I'd definitely keep doing it if my other business ideas don't take off, but if they do take off and they require a little bit more time, this might be put on the back burner, or handed off sooner.

Aha. Let's talk about your other business ideas. What else have you got?

Well, I'm working with a friend on a kind of sustainable banking project. We're trying to figure out a model for a bank that only lends within local communities, and it only lends to sustainable companies and people.

I also have my own other project. Over the summer on one of those days where it's about 120°, I was getting off work at a construction site, building a house. I was watching a ski video and I was thinking, "What if people didn't have to wait in lines, and could pre-purchase their tickets on their phone? Their day tickets or their season passes—what if there was an app for your Smartphone that allowed you to pre-purchase day tickets or season passes and your phone acted as your pass or ticket?"

There's technology at Jay Peak—they're putting it in at Stowe—where you go through this gate, basically, and there's a sensor in the gate and you can have your season's pass, like regular season pass, on your arm or in your pocket and it will sense that you have it and it'll open the gate and let you through. I think it would be a really cool idea if you didn't have to get in line to get a ticket, because god knows, you can be in line for like an hour on those busy days, at least. I was in a line for an hour and a half to try to get my season's pass.

How are you going about moving that idea ahead?

What I really need to do is sit down and hash the specifics: is the app free? Does the app cost money? How does the relationship with the mountain company work? Can I charge them a premium on top of what the customers pay on the date on the season pass? After I hash it out considerably, my next step will be to leverage a relationship with Win Smith, the president of Sugarbush, pitch the idea to him. Hopefully, if he thinks it's a good idea, we'll have a trial one at Sugarbush.

Who are you going to get to do the programming?

There are two possibilities. We have the Emergent Media Center, which is a fantastic resource here on the Champlain College campus. They make Smartphone apps, so I was going to try going to them and working with them. And Scott Baker; my advisor, mentioned to me that he has a very good friend at a social media company called Mullen in Boston and that they do apps, very professional apps, all the time. So if the EMC can't make it happen, I will go to Mullen and see what they can do.

I have to get over the technological hurdle of figuring out how to have it sense that you only have a day pass or you have a season pass, and then I would also have to be building a relationship with the mountains. But if I can do it, then I have the advantage of having a relationship with the mountains, which makes the entry for other competitors very hard.

Interesting. Interesting. So what advice do you have for a 16-year-old student somewhere who's thinking, "Gee, you know, I might want to do something?"

My biggest piece of advice is: just do it. Do a little bit of planning but don't hesitate and sit on it all the time, because that's what most people do— sit on it this idea and it never goes anywhere. You just got to take the initiative.

The golf ball thing was a very simple idea and PaxTunz is more complex, and this app idea, if that launches, is more complex than any of them, but they're building on each other. I'm building on the experiences of each one and taking different things from each one and taking those skills that I learn and combining them to try and reach higher heights every single time.

I guess my second piece of advice would be: you need to be passionate about what you're doing. Don't go see something that you think is profitable but that you have no interest and no passion in and try to go do it.

That's a very good point, but let me ask you: getting that bucket of golf balls and lemonade, where was the passion for you in that?

I did golf and I still golf, so that's a big passion for me. The other thing, I would say, was just being out there in the summer and proving to my parents and proving to myself that I could do it. I was very passionate about that!

▸▸

An important lesson from Paxton's experience is that he has tended to engage in business ideas that, from where he is in his life and with the resources he had, he could actually feasibly implement. Paxton got tremendously valuable experience from, as he says, "just doing it."

You could stand back and say that selling found golf balls and lemonade on a golf course is a pretty simple business, so "What's the big deal?" But Paxton learned a lot about himself, a lot about how to communicate, a bit about marketing and promotion, and he gained a lot of self-confidence in getting a sense that he could really do things. It seems to me that, even through a "simple business," he learned a tremendous amount at a very tender age. In fact, as he says, it was exactly the right enterprise to teach him exactly what he could learn at exactly that age.

The anecdote about selling the entire cart of golf balls shows how much these are coming-of-age stories. At the start of the exchange, the adult is looking to take advantage of the kid and is talking down to him a little. Instead, Paxton looks him (in a manner of speaking) right in the eye and stands up to him, demanding three times what the adult had offered. By the end he has sold his entire cartload and done probably a week's business in a single transaction. And he wraps it up by saying,

"I liked the fact that it was my own blood, sweat, and tears that was making that money." In other words, Paxton didn't see himself as a child any longer: he saw himself as a working adult—in fact, a hard-working adult, working harder, perhaps, than the adults at leisure on the golf course.

Even PaxTunz, while certainly more sophisticated than the golf ball venture, is still a fairly simple business. Paxton had to make an investment of $400 and purchase some equipment, and he had to find facilities, negotiate, test market, and make pricing decisions in the context of his competitive environment and customer target. Paxton faced operational issues—capacity, delivering service levels during peak times. Some of these issues remain to be solved this year, as Paxton anticipates further growth.

Doing these (arguably) smaller and simpler businesses rather than glamorous big dream businesses helped propel Paxton in so many ways, and they have been great preparation for Paxton to create successful big dream businesses in the future.

Paxton Hall 77

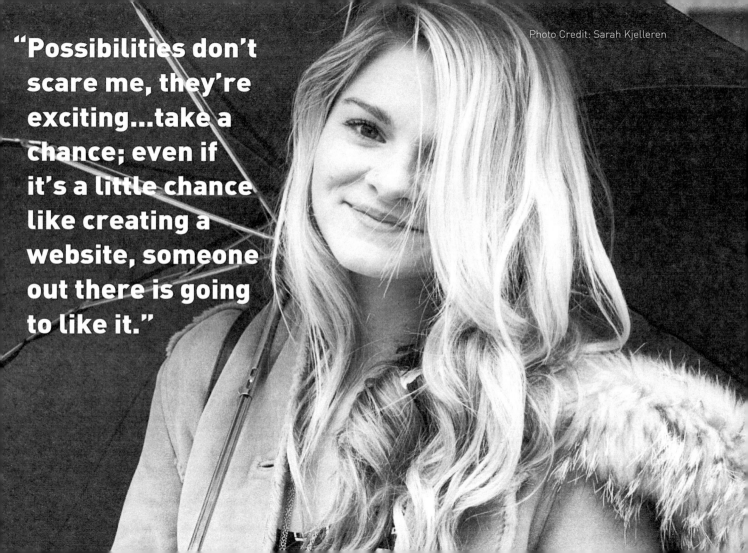

"Possibilities don't scare me, they're exciting...take a chance; even if it's a little chance like creating a website, someone out there is going to like it."

Photo Credit: Sarah Kjelleren

INTERNET TASTEMAKER Molly McGlew

Graphic Design '13 | Hometown: Bedford, NH | Passions: Art, Snowboarding, Fashion | Vixxxen

It seems fitting that I interviewed Molly McGlew by Skype while she was studying in France during her junior year. For one thing, it was only right that she was in the fashion capital of the world, given that she has become something of a tastemaker in one particular field of fashion: the up-and-coming world of snowboarder apparel. For another thing, interviewing her by Skype fits a person who has made a name for herself in digital Internet communications. That name is Vixxxen, a site that has become a go-to for not only snowboarders but makers of snowboard equipment and clothing.

As I understand it, you combine three passions of yours: snowboarding, art and fashion—on a blog, and you've got all kinds of sponsors and are beginning to monetize it in some way.

Yeah. That's pretty much it. I find stuff mostly online—designers' current collections or lookbooks they've released that I like—and then I put them on my website so other people can be introduced to new brands and whatnot. That's the fashion part.

I do the same with snowboarding because snowboarding is similar to fashion in the sense that every season there's new hardware, there's new... everything. It's just the same, it's keeping everybody up to date in one spot with just fashion and snowboarding.

And then the art part. That's just thrown in there just because I'm a graphic design major so I like it.

Fashion's my favorite, then snowboarding, then art, but fashion and snowboarding relate to each other in the sense that they both come out at pretty much the same times and they both have the same ideas behind them. Fashion and snowboarding both are on seasonal rotations—winter collections, fall collections, summer collections for each brand—so I just try to bring those to the forefront for my readers.

When did you start this blog? And what gave you the idea for it? Or did it just evolve?

I started in fall 2010, so it's really new, and it kind of just evolved. My boyfriend, Chas Truslow, goes to Champlain too and he runs a website called The Catfish Chronicles. He's really passionate about snowboarding. So I saw him doing something online, having a blog where he was kind of like a tastemaker, so to speak, on the Internet. He has at least 500 views a day. He just posts videos that he thinks are worthy of showing his friends and his viewers, and like me, he would never post anything he doesn't actually like. In general, he's just a big snowboard nerd! He doesn't do any advertising and sponsorship, all his viewers have been through word of mouth or friends passing his link along, which is amazing!

He finds videos from all over the world on the

Internet and then puts them all in one spot for snowboarders and skateboarders to watch. So he's kind of like a Wikipedia of snowboarding.

He's a content aggregator.

Yes. I saw the positive responses he was getting from his friends and from people online and it made me realize that I could do that exact same thing with my passions. I also was really into websites and blogs so I was like, "You know what? If I can see all these people doing it and being successful, I can make one too."

So you just started it up?

Yeah, exactly. I have always liked playing around with the web. I can't remember exactly when I taught myself but I'm pretty sure it all started around Myspace. In middle school that was the cool thing—everyone wanted their pages to be "like, totally unique." As embarrassing as it is to admit, I think that actually sparked my interest in web design. I like how on the web, you can do whatever you want. There are no creative limits and no one to tell you that you can't do something.

So when I started Vixxxen, I used what I had taught myself earlier on and kept building from there. There were many late nights where my eyes felt like they were going to fall out of my head. As I kept working at it, I would ask my friends who are familiar with web design to guide me or I would just look it up online anytime I was lost.

So I started posting random photos of things that were inspiring such as fashion or art and snowboard videos. It was really simple—just something to browse through.

Just to fill in some background, you're a graphic design major, so when did you start being interested in design or art?

I always have been interested in design and art, from when I first remember. I never really was into graphic design until I came to Champlain. It's a funny story, because as soon as I started doing Vixxxen I realized I'm more into marketing and social media. It's funny how that evolved through Vixxxen as well.

So when you came to Champlain, what were you thinking of studying?

Originally, I was doing marketing, and then my first week of school I switched to graphic design, so I was doing graphic design, and then now, my junior year, I'm back to wanting to do marketing.

Well now you've got me really curious. What happened that first week that made you either decide you didn't want marketing or decide you might like marketing but you just really love graphic design?

The first week of school—my first class of college was at eight o'clock in the morning on a Monday morning and it was a business class with a professor, I don't even remember his name, but he was incredibly boring. I was like, "I need to be in something creative. This is exactly what I don't want to be doing." So after that eight AM class I went to talk to the director of the Graphic Design program, and I was like, "Can I switch?"

But you had to have had some art or design credentials to get into that major, though, right?

I've always been drawing and doing creative stuff and whatnot, like taking tons of art classes in high school but I'd never really done computer stuff until I came to Champlain.

How do you see marketing and art as being connected?

Graphic design and marketing are extremely connected. Right now, for example, I'm in Paris and I look at all the ads. Paris is an international city, obviously, so their ads need to market to everyone. They can't just be for the French people; they have to be for Germans, Americans, Canadians, Russians. They have to be for everybody. I think graphic design comes into place where it's communicating visually instead of just verbally.

That's cool. So you figured all that out by yourself?

Yeah. I'm actually taking my first marketing

class right now, in Paris. I'm a junior, and I've been taking all art classes or graphic design. Now I have the freedom of what I want to take, so I'm taking Communications and International Marketing. It's perfect to be here.

I don't need my degree to say Marketing to know that I'm going to be good at it. As much as that sounds a little cocky, I know I like it and I know I want to do it, so why put myself through more stress switching my major, paying for an extra year of college, when I can take the courses at school and just not have the written part that says marketing?

Yeah. You're good. When I was in high school, I absolutely loved marketing—to the extent I watched TV, I looked at the ads more than the programming and I loved it, I didn't understand why, but I've always loved marketing as a discipline, as something I wanted to do and that's what I did most of my career. Fascinating. So you've taken some unique routes in the path to monetizing your blog. In other words, you don't take ads but you allow people to sponsor you and send you stuff?

Yes. Companies contact me through email. After I made a Twitter, a lot of companies like Nikita and other clothing labels direct messaged me on there as well. Most of the time, those that were interested in working with me would ask if I could help spread the word about a new fashion collection, snowboard video, or even a contest they were putting on.

A couple companies also send me product or clothing and ask that I write a post about it. Mostly, I either get some clothing or product in return or a mention from them on their Facebook page, Twitter, and blogs. That was extremely helpful because it introduced their fans and readers to my blog and exposed me to the public. I think they were interested in working with me because I could reach different types of people and my audience was right for their brands. I never feel like I needed anything in return since everyone I have worked with has been great and helped me get where I am today. People are supportive!

And I guess that way you make your blog more credible, and build more of an audience and a loyal audience. Does that summarize your strategy?

Yes.

Could you talk a little bit about that and your thinking there and how you kind of came to that conclusion?

Basically, I'd rather have support from brands that I support. A lot of times, brands just want to get their advertising space on websites and blogs. They don't really care about what your website is, they just want to make sure it fits their demographic.

They want to know your audience numbers. If you can give them twenty thousand eyeballs, they like you. I gotcha.

Right, so, since my blog was really new, I kind of wanted to not worry about that immediately because I don't need the money from big sponsors; I didn't have these crazy numbers to begin with so my strategy was more of finding companies that I knew would support my website in the beginning and like my ideas, and then help me grow, as opposed to just try to get as many sponsors as I could and having them be useless, not related to me, I tried to get people that I knew would support me and genuinely be interested.

Now my sponsors usually send me monthly newsbytes with all of their upcoming events, collection launches, and exclusive content. In general it is nice to have, since I usually hear about things first. I can often post it before other blogs and help spread the word early. They also hook me up with some great connections—people to meet or general advice and suggestions. And I've gotten random gifts from them too, which is always a plus! Who doesn't love a free pair of shoes arriving at their doorstep?

For my part, I write the articles, spread the news, and promote the company as a whole. It can be a lot of work, but it is completely worth it. I get a lot of support and have made some great connections with companies I have always admired.

And you've correctly figured out that in any kind of a media, be it a magazine or anything, even a TV show, your sponsors are part of the programming.

Yeah. I would get companies' contacts, emails, and search and search and search for them, or I would ask people if they had a podcast, or kind of use connections I just invented to get their emails, and then just be like, "Hey, I started this website; check it out when you have time; yada yada yada," and they would respond and be like, "We're into it," and then I would ask if they would want to be associated with it as a "supporter," because I think a supporter sounds like it's more on a friend basis than a sponsor. I went with that word because, I just always thought "sponsor" sounds sort of superficial; "supporter" sounds more genuine; I went with that theme. So that's kind of how it happened—I just kind of put myself out there.

So you got the whole networking thing. You said, "I'm going to go out there, find these people, and I'm going to approach them and I don't care what they think about me. I'm not going to be shy, I'm just going to go out there."

Exactly. And what's the worst thing they'll say: No? Or not email me back, you know?

You say that like it's so obvious but there's so many people, people of all ages, who would just be terrified to do that.

Yeah. I don't know. It's not like they can see my face, and it's not like I'm asking them in person anyways; obviously that's more intimidating. If you're hiding behind a computer screen, you should have no fear when you're asking for something—just go for it.

So how do you develop your audience— and how big an audience do you have?

When you are passionate about something, you want to work really, really hard at it. I love blogging and introducing people to new things; it feels like my little contribution to the world. I think that it is extremely important to connect with your readers and other companies you support on a personal level.

I always check my Google Analytics every night to see what other website are talking about me and sending people to my blog. It helps me connect with the people who have the same interests and who enjoy my blog and what I have to say. It's also cool to see what countries they are coming from and what specific types of posts people enjoy most.

Here's a quick tip: if you are a blogger or run a website, get Google Analytics! It shows you what countries people are coming from; it shows you everything. I have at least 250 viewers a day, though it varies depending on certain posts and how they're presented, and it also depends on the season. If it's during the school year, it's much more. In the summer, fewer people are on the Internet. On average, I have around 6,000 views a month. My best day to date was when I had 1,200 views in one day after posting an article with Burton. It was amazing!

That's cool, very cool. And what are your goals for this thing?

Basically, I'm just rolling with it and going with the flow for right now, because whatever I've been doing, I've been doing right. So I don't want to try to do something that I'm uncomfortable with, because I've had a lot of great opportunities so far with me just doing what I've been doing.

My higher hopes for Vixxxen are that I would love to have it be more visible to more people. I'd love to just be kind of a tastemaker in the snowboarding or fashion industry in general. That's my ideal dream so this is my little chunk of the Internet where I can do that.

That's cool; now do companies like Burton chase after you?

I actually got in touch with Burton—specifically, Amanda Wormann, their marketing guru. I got in touch with her one day and said, "I have this idea. Let me know if you're interested. I would love to do a tour of the Burton factory and document it on my website, and just kind of do a factory-girl, behind-the-scenes kind of post."

She was actually really down for it and she took me on this private tour with another guy who knew everything about Burton and I got 2,000 views the day I posted that, so that was pretty unreal.

So you'll be back to them, probably?

I'll talk to them again soon, hopefully. That was cool; such a well-known company turned out to be really, really inviting, welcoming. That was awesome.

What do you think it is about you that enables you to do this thing?

I've always been a creative person, but, for instance graphic design is hard for me because I have ideas in my brain and things I want to do, but I can't get them out in design specifically. I think that Vixxxen is my creative outlet. And I've always liked writing but I've never been a writer, so I get to lay out everything on my blog: I get to design all the logos, how I want everything, then I get to write the articles, I have entire creative control over the entire thing, and to me that is crucial.

I think that might be why it sticks out a little— because it's very, very much me, as opposed to being a blog about snowboarding or a blog about fashion that's supposed to appeal to other people. It's more for my own benefit. I like what I post and I believe in what I post, even if it's just a necklace that I like. I never post or write about anything that I wouldn't own myself or I wouldn't wear myself, so I guess it's just kind of a taste thing. Maybe people like my taste but it's definitely just overall my creative outlet; it's my space on the Internet.

That is really interesting. So, if you were talking to a bunch of 16 year olds, what would you say? What advice would you give them as they're wondering what to do with their lives?

First, I always knew I was going to do something that was very independent. I think it depends on a person but the whole "Just Do It" slogan—I really believe in that, because seriously, I just did it and went for it and made a blog and I found out it's my passion. So if you even have a hunch that you might like something or even think that you could potentially be good at something, why not try it and just do it?

It's like you said before: what's the worst that can happen?

Exactly.

It's so amazing; when you say that, it sounds so obvious but it's so hard for so many people.

I know, and I think people are scared of possibilities. Possibilities don't scare me, they're exciting, so I don't understand why people just don't take a chance—even if it's a little chance like creating a website, someone out there is going to like it. Whether it's one person or whether it's 20 million people, someone can enjoy what you have to say and I just think that's really inspiring.

You have a semester in Paris, right?

Yep. I'm studying at CEA, a third-party study abroad group. The classes are all in English but I'm taking French as well. And the outside, the city is my classroom. It's great. I love it.

A woman I met through a snowboard company actually emailed me before I left and introduced me to people I should meet while living in Paris. I took her advice, met up with a few people, and we actually became great friends! Little connections like that would have never been possible without Vixxxen, and it is absolutely amazing.

I have also found a lot of French clothing brands that I have featured on the site, and then got in contact with them. I was actually invited to their showroom to meet the designers and see the clothing in a private setting. Being in Europe has definitely given me great opportunities and I still have plenty more time to explore Europe! New friends in a new city—what is a better gift than that?

The fact is, in my work I meet many young people like Molly. They have the energy and they relish the delight and excitement of creation. Some people shy away from starting up their own business because they're afraid it will be too much work, or take too much time, but the sheer act of having the idea and putting it into effect gives her tremendous amounts of energy, which in turn makes her magnetic.

Notice also the irrelevance of money. She isn't wealthy and has no start-up capital. What she has is ideas, energy, and the desire to make them real. Those qualities in themselves are her capital, and when the right time comes they will attract funding.

A couple of other points: the promise of entrepreneurship is not so much that you'll make a fortune but that you'll be able to spend your life doing what you like to do. That's exactly how Molly started, and that in itself takes a huge risk: we're usually encouraged to do what we think other people will want us to do, not what we ourselves want.

A second effect that follows on from this initial courage is that when we see people acting with courage, we recognize it instantly, and we react differently to them. They become leaders—or, in her language, tastemakers. Nobody follows a coward.

"Everything is creative in business when you're the entrepreneur."

MOVING UP THROUGH THE GEARS Jonathan Fischer

Business '11 | Hometown: Lunenburg, MA | Passion: Skiing | Wireless ESP, LLC d.b.a Speedbump

There are many good reasons for Jon Fischer to be cocky and arrogant. But the Jon Fischer you meet is so quiet and unassuming you would never learn about any of them. Massachusetts state robotics champion in middle school, a nationally ranked junior freestyle skier with Olympic ambitions (until he blew out a knee), winner of big cash prizes in "adults included" business plan competitions while still in high school—you might be able to pry the admission of those achievements out of Jon, but it would take a good amount of effort.

Of course, hang around him long enough and you will witness that piercing gleam in his eyes that provides a hint of the fierce competitive spirit within.

Jon's entrepreneurial journey is fascinating, rooted in a strong curiosity about technology and fueled by his love of building things and his competitive spirit. It features a family that seemed to know how to be supportive, while giving Jon the room to struggle a bit and make things his own.

Jon's business, Speedbump, grew out of a high school science project, has gone through several major iterations as underlying technology has changed, and now is at another major crossroads.

Let's go back to the early days, when you were working with a robotics club—in middle school?

I guess I really started showing interest in technology in the First Lego League, which was the robotics middle school league. I was Massachusetts state champion three years in a row. Loved doing that. I was really into tech.

The Lego robot was for the first Lego League. Each year the league would design a unique "competition table" that would have a variety of tasks for the robot to do. These tasks would be mainly to interact with certain objects on the table (close or open gates, push buttons) or have the robot deliver one object to a specified place on the table. All of these tasks would be worth points and the more you could have your robot get done in the allotted time, the better you ranked. My team was State Champions three times and one year we placed second in the Nationals.

So, you were on a team? In that robotics league?

Well, I founded it, and got a lot of friends to do it with me. We did a lot on both sides of building—the hardware of the Legos, and the programming. We actually had a lot of good hacks in there, and subroutines. You're only allowed to have five programs run when the robot goes out on the table, but we actually had a secret hack that got us through inspection, because we used a touch sensor to hide multiple programs inside one.

What do you think was the attraction of playing around with code and robotics and all that?

I always loved Legos, and just building things, and I thought that this whole idea sounded really awesome. It was competitive too, which was really cool. So you spend a lot of time building physical things, and that's where I really learned to program a little bit.

And you were also developing as a skier at this time too, right?

Yes. I would ski a lot recreationally. Then, in seventh grade, I really started getting into freestyle skiing, and started to compete. I spent a lot of time focusing on that, and then that really became huge in high school, and I got sponsored and traveled all across the country competing, which was fantastic.

And I've seen this one picture of you doing this outrageous aerial. So you were one of those guys that was leaping off those ramps, and going 60 feet in the air, and flipping all over the place and all that?

Yup, yup.

Wow, so you were an athlete and a geek at the same time.

Absolutely, and I loved the mix. It was great.

Did your parents have any role in all this, or did you stumble on this yourself?

Well, my dad had been an entrepreneur and had had a few companies, so I guess I had the idea that I would want to start a company some day in the back of my mind. But other than just being really supportive in whatever I really was interested in, they didn't play a big role.

Compared to your friends, what would you say was your level of curiosity and your willingness and eagerness to try new things? Where do you think that trait comes from?

I couldn't tell you where it comes from, but I guess it was pretty high. What I noticed was that once I put my mind to something I tend to keep following down that path instead of just being really into something for maybe a week or a month and then moving on.

So then you're on to high school—and the robots, did you keep doing that in high school?

No, I didn't. Our school couldn't afford to keep that up, because it's about 20 times more expensive to run a high school program.

Okay, so what did you gravitate to in high school?

The first couple years of high school, I focused more on skiing than on continuing to build things, at least any serious projects. But when I was a junior, I wanted to do something in the Massachusetts state science fair.

I was going for my driver's license at this time, and had a couple friends who had gotten into small fender benders, and one friend had actually crashed his car and injured himself and two friends. This made me angry, because I knew it was a preventable crash: they were excessively speeding, on a small back road. And that's what led to Speed Demon, which became Speedbump.

Speed Demon was a hardware device for teen driving safety. Speedbump is my new product that is a smart phone app for teen driving safety. Speedbump turns a teen's smartphone into a driving safety sensor and brings parents and teens together to promote safe driving. The app will report on dangerous driving. If a teen drives safely it will never send reports. The report opens a dialogue between parents and teens on how to improve teen driving and lets parents relax a bit more when their teen is out with the car.

I started working on the project for the science fair and made the first prototype, in which I developed some of the algorithms for the patents that I would later file.

Where did those come from? How did you learn how to do that?

Well, I guess the middle school Lego robotics. Even though the programming was much simpler, it helped with understanding how logic functions work, and how you can kind of define the logic that you're looking for. That definitely carried over and gave me a leg up.

But Speed Demon, the thing for the science fair—I guess you added a way to use the data that spewed out by the GPS unit to give you some useful information about what speed was suitable to the road conditions, right?

Right, but not necessarily road conditions. We called them road classes. You'd break roads down into three road classes: local or neighborhood roads, which are the really small, small roads; secondary roads, that are in between the local roads and the highways; and then actual highways.

Before I began working on how to use GPS information to figure out what type of road you're driving on, I did an analysis of the Fatal Accident Reporting System from the National Highway Traffic Safety Administration. I proved that for teen drivers it's incredibly more dangerous to speed on local and secondary roads than it is on highways. It's not that speeding on highways is good, but 75 mph in a 65 mph zone is far less dangerous than 50 in a 40 zone, even though in both cases it's only 10 mph over the speed limit. That's because the back roads have much poorer visibility, and far more corners.

So you're going to the science fair with this kind of crude prototype, and you win...

I didn't win, actually. I got an honorable mention. But a couple of people at the science fair, even some of the judges, said, "I've got kids in high school, too—that would be a great product some day." And I was thinking, "This definitely isn't ready to be a product, but maybe some day." And my dad was like, "Hey, you could probably try to do a business plan competition."

Interesting. So a little consumer feedback got you encouraged. And you went to a business plan competition? That was your attempt to try and commercialize it?

Yeah, to try to commercialize it, to learn more about business, and to see if I could make a working business model out of it. And actually, it did work pretty well. I came up with a whole marketing plan, a manufacturing plan, over the summer between my junior and senior year of high school at the Olympic Training Center at Lake Placid, where I was training for my illustrious skiing career.

So hold on for a second here. What did the other skiers think of this? They're all sitting around after practice, I don't know what they're doing, but they're probably

not developing a business plan. What did they think of you developing this business plan?

They thought it was kind of funny, especially because most of them were my age. Some of them didn't really like the concept of a safety product for teen driving. Actually that's part of my peer feedback—that's why I developed a product that I feel is designed to work for teens and parents equally. The whole premise has been that Speedbump or Speed Demon will never report back to parents unless the teen is driving dangerously. So as long as they stay safe, they're in the clear.

And you built that into the business plan for this competition?

Absolutely. That was included in the whole marketing plan. There were actually a couple devices out there that were kind of rudimentary, repurposed GPS systems where you could kind of just constantly record, and were designed to just kind of sneak into your teen's car and spy on them. And in my marketing section of

the business plan, I talked a lot about how my product is meant to open the dialogue between parents and teens, and not act as a spying device. To honestly say, "We trust you, just drive safe, and this will prove it, and then we won't track you or anything like that."

And I entered it in the first annual Mount Wachusett Community College Business Plan Competition. Which wasn't just for the college, it was for anybody in Massachusetts. Actually, I don't think it was even limited to Massachusetts.

So you go to this business plan competition and you win. What were you thinking when you came up to the podium to get your award?

I was really excited. I couldn't really believe it. I was definitely the youngest person pitching. There were a couple of college students but there were also quite a few middle-aged entrepreneurs and entrepreneurs who had already run a successful company. So I was incredibly pumped that I won almost $20,000, half in prizes and half in cash. I used that to incorporate, file the patents, get a new computer for the business, and kind of got rolling.

That's when it really solidified that I really wanted to do the business and actually go for it. So that was in the fall my senior year of high school. In the spring I started looking for schools and also started applying for scholarships. I won the National Federation of Independent Businesses "Plan for the Future" competition. I think that was another $10,000 for the business. I also got entrepreneurial scholarships from the McKelvey Foundation, and Champlain College, and another $2,000 dollar scholarship from the NFIB.

What were you doing the rest of senior year?

The big thing for me was to try and get some exercise first, and then do the work. I always felt I was better at getting my work done—one, better quality, and two, more efficiently—if I go outside first and do something that's really just sport or hobby. After that, I can settle down and focus and get things done that might not be quite as exciting as hitting jumps on skis, but definitely still exciting.

During my senior year, when I saw how much success I was having in the business plan arena and with young entrepreneur recognition, I realized I wanted to take more of a business path than a technical path, and decided to go for business at college instead of computer science.

Was that because you found you were more inherently interested in the business side, or because you were getting more positive feedback in the business side?

I enjoyed the business aspect more. I didn't expect starting a business to be a creative endeavor, but it is, actually. Marketing strategies, and even just monetization strategies—everything is creative in business when you're the entrepreneur, as opposed to just working in a large corporation.

So tell me, what was it like at Champlain your first year?

It was great until December 11, when I blew out

my knee sliding a handrail through the middle of campus. Then it was pretty awful for the rest of that year, because I was on crutches. I was really upset, and I lost my ski sponsors. But because skiing wasn't my only interest, I continued to drive towards the business even harder.

It took me until the summer between the sophomore and junior years of school to launch Speed Demon, which was the hardware version.

By hardware version you mean the little black box that you would put under the dashboard, the recording device that sent the data back, right?

Right. And one really important part of getting that done was finding partnerships. In business I have found that strategic alliances are super important, the most important thing. It is much better than trying to take everyone head on, and think of everyone as a competitor. In an entrepreneurial sense, being driven to succeed isn't necessarily competitive like sports are. There's not necessarily a clear-cut winner and loser. You can get symbiotic relationships going that are mutually beneficial, and that's always been huge.

My first big lesson was realizing that even though I'd won close to $30,000 in business plan competitions for getting my business started, for manufacturing your own hardware GPS, that amount of capital was not even close to enough. Not even a fraction of the way there. I ended up getting a contact at Fastrax in Finland who made a hardware box that actually had pretty much the specs I needed, which they were developing to branch the market. It just happened to be a good platform for what would be my hardware product. They actually paid me and my company to do consulting work, which was testing their firmware on that device. So they pretty much paid 90 percent of the development of my first product, because we were helping them get their firmware ready to start commercializing their product.

So they had some cool technology, but they didn't really have an application for it, so they could test it. You provided an

application. Did their product have the GPS unit in it, and also the telecommunications unit in it?

Yes, that's what their box was. It was called the uTrace. It had both a SIM card slot, and the GPS, and a microprocessor in it. So it had all the actual hardware that we needed, and they wanted to sell it because it was designed to be used for a wide variety of applications, running their own custom firmware that you could kind of build your own application on top of. They had trouble developing a really bulletproof firmware, which is how we got involved. We started finding bugs for them, and said, "Well we don't know if we want to develop on your platform if it's gonna be this buggy." And they said, "Well why don't we pay you to just keep working on it?" And we said, "Sure, why not?"

That took us another 18 months to really get ready to go to market. This was going into my junior year and we launched right into the whole recession, which didn't really help. We sold about 50 Speed Demons total, which was good considering that Fast Track was great. We never

paid them out of pocket. We'd never have been able to get over those costs.

What was really interesting, though, was that I wasn't selling nearly as many as I hoped. The parents that had it, they all loved it, and they really felt like it was making their teens safer drivers, which was great. And I think one of the great things about being an entrepreneur is having people use a product that you design, and that you are responsible for creating is a really cool feeling, especially when they give you such positive feedback on it.

So what I learned was that a lot of parents said they were interested, but they couldn't really afford the $200 hardware, and then the subscription—especially considering that teen drivers are really only teen drivers for about eighteen months before that college transition. So it was costing like, $40 a month, as opposed to $20. So that was too much.

So you ran into a real barrier to purchase? To the customer, the economics of it was hard for them to swallow?

Right. So I was starting to get a little concerned. The marketing wasn't really working as well as I had hoped. One night I was hanging out with a couple of my friends, playing with one of my friends' new iPhone, seeing all the apps on it, what it could do, and I realized, "Wait, I don't need to sell hardware any more." Smartphones have everything in there that you need. If the up-front cost is the one big problem that's making parents not want the product, why not just get rid of it, and just move to Smartphones?

In other words, if the Smartphone has GPS, it has the telecommunications, and it's going to be carried by the person, you don't have to buy another box—you just have to download your app. Interesting. So you discovered that one night, and then what did you do?

I really thought I had something. I researched it a little more, and decided that it was exactly what we needed to do. The idea behind the app was that it should really not have to be activated and turned on by the teen, it should kind of just hang out in the background, and make sure everything was okay. And that's why we tried to go to Android first, and we beta-tested on Android just as I was about to graduate.

And at this point you had a few software professionals, who were helping you either part time or full time to help you do the development work, right?

Absolutely. And part of that first relationship actually came from one of my dad's friends utilizing his network to get a guy who worked for me part time at the beginning. He had done contracting work for that first company, and we pretty much took him on, and I was paying him pretty much all of that contracting money back to him, just to get the product built with his expertise. I did have some coding experience, but it wasn't really practical. I never had the skill level to make a real product.

Then you're graduating, and then you make a big decision to go for the MassChallenge. So why don't you talk about that?

I knew I wanted to stay full time on my business when I got out of school, because everything was really coming together as I graduated. There's always more to learn, and I wasn't afraid to admit that I still wanted mentors.

So that really inspired me to get into MassChallenge, which is still the world's largest start-up accelerator competition. It's based in south Boston, and it's a three-month program where 125 finalists this year got free office space, and tons of mentorship, and all kinds of programs related to marketing, user experience, business, and working with investors. Pretty much everything start-up.

So I was one of those 125 companies that got free office space. I think close to 800 applied, so that was a huge win just in itself, just getting in there. And I continued to learn so much. In two weeks, it's the beginning of final judging. Sixteen teams out of that 125 will win either $100,000 or $50,000, and I've been working on my pitch like crazy.

So you've got a lot on the line. When they judge, how much is based on the progress you made, or is it just on your presentation?

I think it's 50/50. Half is to show how much you have done in the last three months, to show that building of momentum, how MassChallenge helped you. The other half just on the presentation, and how realistic is your business model is—do they actually believe that you will succeed? And I mean, it's not going to be exactly the same pitch that you would give to investors, but it's pretty close, because really they're putting those dollars to work with you. Even though they're a nonprofit, they want those teams they pick to win and really create jobs.

Just some crazy stats: the 100 companies they took last year for the first MassChallenge, in the nine months since they've graduated, they've raised a total of over $90 million from outside money, and created over 400 jobs. So it's really an honor even to get into that level.

Well, good luck in that. Any final words or wisdom for some high school student

who's got an idea or dream?

You'll never know what happens with your idea unless you try to go for it. If you don't follow through and really try to make it happen, it won't. So you might as well try.

And what's the most important thing as you're trying it?

Stay with it. You're definitely going to hit some speed bumps through the process, but you can overcome them, and good things will happen.

▸▸

Jon and Speedbump are at a crossroads. Jon failed to win at MassChallenge. It seems another start up in the space had taken a different technological approach, had more market momentum, and edged Jon out of the winner's circle. However, he is still working with his mentors at the program to explore the options of an outside investment to grow the company.

Jon has learned much and accomplished a great deal in his young life. His personal growth has been phenomenal. Particularly fascinating to me is how his passion and creative outlet has morphed from one rooted in technology to one rooted in business and marketing. It may be premature to make this comparison, but in this respect Jon's path, in terms of his true passion, is remarkably similar to the late Steve Jobs, who started as a true "geek" building those crude early Apple computers with Steve Wozniak, but realized his greatest triumphs as arguably the ultimate marketer and business strategist of the last two decades.

"I have just always been a very assertive person."

THE MIME'S DAUGHTER Marguerite Dibble

Game Art & Animation '12 | Hometown: North Landgrove, VT | Passion: Telling Stories | Birnamwood Games

If you happen to see Marguerite Dibble striding across campus with her long legs, fashion-forward look, and "out there" earrings, you might conclude she was a supermodel late for a photo shoot. A good guess, but you would be wrong. Marguerite is nothing less than a creative force to be reckoned with.

I first met Marguerite four years ago at an on-campus open house for prospective students. We discussed some small businesses she was operating, but she quickly turned the conversation to bigger dreams she had for her future. Today, as her nascent game company nears the release of its first game, *Loc*, on the iPad platform, business issues are moving to the forefront of Marguerite's mind.

From my perspective, Marguerite has engaged in business matters with the same gusto as the creative side. Raise issues of financing strategy, she's all ears. Suggest that she attend local entrepreneurial networking events to learn to practice pitching her business to potential investors, and she's there working the room. What I have learned since we first met is that Marguerite Dibble is not just a dreamer. She's a doer, a creative person with great entrepreneurial instincts, drive, and leadership skills.

When was the first time in your life that you were doing anything that can even remotely be described as entrepreneurial or your own business, your own thing?

Very, very early on. It's just sort of how I've always been. It's come out in different ways. When I was in preschool I organized everyone into a theatre company and directed and wrote things. I've just always been a very assertive person: I started talking before I was one and would go to grown-up dinner parties and have full conversations with people when I was about two, talking about things I wanted to do and ideas and stuff. That just sort of carried through—I mean, not necessarily on the business front because when you're little you don't really know that exists yet, but when I was in third grade I created my own religion based on the idea of multiple compact universes inside of microscopic atomic space..

Then I did a lot of personal theatre projects and writing projects, just telling stories—because that's what I've always been interested in: telling stories that people can experience in new and interesting ways, and tying that into philosophy and big ideas about human beings and stuff like that.

As I got older and history moved forward or what have you, video games really came into my life a lot because video games are this fantastic new way to tell stories: they're interactive, they get people to learn in an amazing way that communicates so clearly. Gabe Newell, who's the president of Steam, an international online game distribution company that carries both independent- and major-label games, did a talk where he described giving a two-year-old child a video game, and even though this kid wasn't even interacting with other people in a real way yet, the child learned the video game because of how good games are at communicating skills. They really touch something deep inside about how we learn and develop, so it's really a perfect platform for taking great stories and communicating them to people in an accessible, modern way.

What else were you doing along the way?

There's been a lot of stuff. When I was in seventh grade, I taught myself how to use Photoshop because I thought it would be a valuable skill, and it turned out to be one of the best, smartest things I ever could have done for myself because I've done freelance graphic design, which is sort of like owning your own company; you're pushing yourself out for small jobs for other people. I've been doing that since I was in about eighth grade and that's helped pay a lot of bills. I tried to use design other ways that I didn't realize were totally not viable before then. Like, when I was like 11, I bought a pin making machine—like campaign buttons—and I would take pictures from comic books and I would make them into buttons and I would sell them online, which was lucrative until someone pointed out to me that it was very illegal, which I didn't realize [*laughs*] so I didn't do that anymore. Then I designed T-shirts for a while at the end of high school and sold those for a while, and now I'm doing freelance graphic designs.

Artistry and creativity in everything you've done. Where does that come from?

That's totally from my family. My dad actually went to college to be a mime and lived in Boston without shoes for four years doing mime in leotards in the park, because he cared about theatre. I grew up with a lot of theatre people.

So you came up to Champlain with your T-shirt company, and then you started discovering other stuff. I know just in the time we've known each other you've had a magazine, and then a game venture we'll talk about.

I've always written stories as well as just coming up with things. I wrote a 600 page novel that isn't as long as it should be. Maybe in the next couple years I'll be able to have the patience to go back and make it probably the 3,000 pages that it should be—and various comic books, graphic novel scripts, 300 page graphic novels that I can submit at some point. All various forms of stories, a lot of the ideas of which drain into stuff that I'm doing now.

The magazine is actually something I had a lot of fun with and would like to be able to go back to once I'm more capable of doing it. It's still up on the web, and I'm going to keep it up, keep paying for the web hosting until I can start working on it again. The magazine was called *Arrant Knaves*, but the main idea was in the subtitle, which was, "For the polymath in all of us." As we enter this new millennium we sort of have this funny Renaissance thing that's going on. People have so many interests. You find people who are really into history and express that through sketchy web comics, or people who love classic literature but also enjoy a good action movie, and we have these collisions of the classical and the modern, and gender roles that don't really apply anymore.

I got so irritated with the magazines that are available for women. *Glamour* and *Cosmopolitan* and *Vogue*. They're pretty shallow—but in many ways the male magazines are just as shallow, with work-out schedules and diet plans and cars and stuff. So the idea is to be able to combine a lot of things that everyone can care about, then add some deeper elements like things you might find inside *Harper's*, or philosophy, literature, and history—but also film and fashion and more modern pursuits, for these people whose interests are broad, like mine are.

We did four issues; I had to stop doing it because they were 50 pages each and I was writing 90 percent of that material. I had a couple people who were helping me out. Rafi Diaz, who was a Champlain student, wrote my tech articles and my game articles, and he's been egging me to get it going again, so we'll see. I had a friend of mine from Bennington College do some fashion articles, and then I did the rest, which was 85 to 90 percent; I did all of the graphic design for all of the pages.

So, I did all of that and I also did all of the web publishing so I had to do the HTML code and push it up onto the website. It was something that I really enjoyed. I feel the motivations behind the project still hold true and still have an audience, so in the future, once I'm actually able to feed myself, I'll have to go back. There are some new applications that have come out since that would make it much more profitable.

So tell us about Birnamwood Games—where it is right now, how it happened, how it's developed, who's on your team, where you see it going.

The whole idea of the game company sort of started about a year ago. My boyfriend—we've been together for many years—went to Boston for a couple months because he'd just gotten out of school and there was an engineering job opportunity there that he was interested in. I went to visit him a couple times and I was like, "God, I don't really like this city too much." I grew up in Vermont, I love Vermont, I think it's a great place and I said, "You know what? I want to make something happen here."

Burlington is a great place to make something happen, especially with video-gaming, because it's right between Montreal and Boston and those are two big areas for games. If it's so close to both those, there's no reason why it can't happen here. There are a lot of big media houses such as JDK in Burlington, and that's a similar sort of field, so last year I said, "I'm going to make this happen."

Here's what I am doing. I'm starting a company here, and it's going to be about doing artistic games that are accessible and simple but communicate something more. I asked Zach Bohn, who's a game designer at Champlain I'd done things with before. He was actually in Montreal at the time but he was interested, he said yes. I talked to a programmer, Michael Hopke, a Champlain student who always had intelligent things to say when we were discussing philosophy and always got his homework in on time, so I took those as positive signs.

It started out as just us for a while, brainstorming about what we wanted to do. We initially were thinking about doing a much larger game, similar to the stuff that you see on gaming consoles like Xbox and PlayStation. But as I did more research into the industry and what's wanted and what's available now, I saw that mobile gaming on cell phones has opened up this huge door: anyone can be a mobile gamer, no matter their gender or age or anything, if they have a phone and they want to spend some time on it. That's an audience, so we decided that we would go for smaller, simpler games that had depth, but that were easy to play and easy to use and easier for us to make because they were a smaller scale.

Our first game, *Loc*, is based off a prototype that Zach made in Montreal as an experiment. It's a very visual, spatial reasoning game so it's hard to explain the concept exactly, but the idea is basically that there's a four by four grid and on this grid sit tiles; there's a tile that's the end of a road and there's a tile that's the start of a road and there are some other tiles that are pieces of a road and you slide the tiles around the grid in order to connect the end to the beginning in a consistent path.

That's the very simple version, but how it gets complex is that this road actually travels over six faces of a cube, so you have to carry this path around three-dimensional corners, back and forth, through tiles that can't be moved—so the idea is that you take a simple two-dimensional concept that anyone can grasp easily and you broaden it to three dimensions as something that's mentally exciting.

Underneath that we have a narrative that reflects some of our goals as a company to incorporate classical, artistic, philosophical ideas.

Where are you now in terms of development?

Right now we're pretty much done. We built it on the computer first. That's the easiest thing for us to do, especially since we're a start-up and we don't have any income right now, so we use our own resources, which are our own personal computers, to build it. Now we're just testing it on people to make sure the puzzles aren't too hard, to make sure they have everything people want as players.

Our goal is to have our game totally finished by the end of October 2011 because we'll be submitting it to a large independent game contest with Game Developers Conference, the big game industry conference out in California, and the deadline for that is the end of October. Then we'll spend the next two months putting it on our first device to sell it. The iPad is going to be our first selling platform. And that'll be for Christmas.

The game's going to be priced at $2. The publisher takes 30 percent. It'd be nice if we could have a little bit more than $1 per game, and two bucks is a nice price point, because it's cheap—it's like the fact that during the recession, candy bar sales went up because it's a cheap thing that makes me feel good and I can have access to. We're using the same sort of marketing trick.

So, what advice would you share with teenager who's thinking, "Gee, I'd like to do something on my own some day"?

I would say, be discerning. Think about what there's a need for, why what you're going to do is special and how you're going to make people see that it's special. That's really important. You have to have a market or else it's not going to be worth it. You have to be able to have something that when you talk to people about it, their eyes light up and they go, "Oh, really?" or, like, "Oh, that sounds kind of cool," and they get excited.

I would also say listening to other people is a gigantic part of being successful at anything. One of the reasons our team works so well together is we all make up the game. We have a designer, and I'm the creative director, or whatever, but when we go in and we pitch the idea, everyone's ideas have value—they build video games, they obviously play video games, so of course their opinions matter. Being able to talk to people about it, seeing what they think, and taking their input and actually applying it is really vital.

Advice is huge. I wouldn't be where I was at all if I didn't realize, "Okay, I don't know very much at all about the business end of things so I'm going to talk to people who know about it, really listen to them, get their feedback, take what they say seriously, because they know more about it than I do, and just do my best to listen and learn and take it to heart and then go with that."

▸▸

Marguerite is a young woman who is remarkably self-aware. She has her own view of the world, and it drives her to want to make things happen.

She knows what she likes to do and what she is good at doing. The sheer act of having the idea and putting it into effect gives her tremendous amounts of energy, which in turn makes her magnetic. People listen to her because they instinctively recognize that energy and that sense of purpose.

But what separates her—and most of the students in this book—from many of her peers is that they have no reservations about jumping in and trying things, doing things, following through. It's a big reason why they are likely to succeed as entrepreneurs. Marguerite is perfectly comfortable taking charge, organizing things, suggesting to other people how they can take part. Again, that's empowering: people (including backers, investors, collaborators) respond best to someone who is comfortable as a leader.

What Marguerite is doing in terms of financing Birnamwood Games is demonstrative of a strategy young companies can use when start-up funds are low. Marguerite has chosen the path of many entrepreneurs, "bootstrapping" her company

with limited capital until she can release her first game, and prove to potential investors that her company can deliver a commercially viable game. She accomplished this by having the entire team forego any salaries during this phase, and performing all the game development work in the Champlain Game Lab. Of course, the company will have to purchase commercial software licenses prior to the game's release, a $5,000 investment. For this money, Marguerite is counting on a loan from her family.

To make Birnamwood Games a good career alternative for her team, Marguerite will offer them modest salaries, plus the opportunity to earn a significant ownership position in the company with continued performance over time. The challenge for Marguerite is to structure these employee-ownership-plans so that there is good alignment between employees' expectations and the company's need for these key employees to stay and produce over time. This will mean an initial grant of stock to these key players upon release of Game 1. Once Game 1 is released on the iPad, the plan is for the team to complete work on a second and third game.

A final note on Marguerite. While she is becoming very involved with financial issues, it is clear that for Marguerite, Birnamwood Games is not about the money. It is more about the pure unadulterated joy of creating something that lives and breathes and provides a value—in this case, entertainment—to others. This motivation is something she shares with all the other young entrepreneurs in this book.

"I know how it works, to be an orphan child. So, if I can put that bad experience to good use, that would really make more sense."

TAKING FLIGHT Peter Garang Deng

Business '11 | Hometown: Bor Village, South Sudan | Passion: Helping the People of His Home Country
New Sudan Jonglei Orphans Foundation & Peter Eagle Transporation Company

I have been fortunate to meet many inspiring young people in my time at Champlain, but few have inspired me as much as Peter Garang Deng. Peter was born into the Dinka tribe in a little village in South Sudan. He lost both parents by the age of five, and was taken in by relatives but endured ill-treatment and neglect. Despite all this, Peter somehow managed to survive and eventually thrive. His struggle to exist as a young child by finding ways to entertain his more fortunate classmates (and get himself invited to their homes for a meal), his harrowing journey to Kenya and existence in the notorious refugee camps, his eventual journey to the United States, and to graduate from Champlain College is the stuff of a good feature film.

Peter first came to me for help starting his non-profit, the New Sudan Jonglei Orphans Foundation (NSJOF). His vision was simple: just as his own life had been transformed by education, NSJOF would raise money to educate as many orphans as possible in South Sudan at good schools, so that they in turn could grow to be productive citizens and give back to their people.

Recently, Peter has developed a new idea to accelerate the pace of growth of NJSOF's impact. But first, here's Peter's tale in his own words.

If you look back in your life, where do you think that entrepreneurship started with you?

Well, it started when I was an orphan child, when my parents passed away. My mother passed away from disease when I was only eight months old, and my father died when I was five years old. In the years following my father's death, my sisters and I moved back and forth between my aunt's family and my uncle's family, who would beat me and refuse to feed me.

So I went through a difficult life, and I didn't give up. I did all the best I can to be who I am today. Finally realizing that I could turn that bad experience around and use it to give back to the people in my community—that's where my power as an entrepreneur came from.

Your father passed away when you were five, but in some ways, even though he was only with you for a short time, he had a tremendous effect on you.

When he knew he wouldn't live much longer, he would say, "Listen to me. When you grow up you have to do something for this village."

I would ask, "How am I going to do something for this village? I am too young, I don't even understand what you're talking about."

"Listen," he said. "If you help somebody today, that person will turn around and help another person who is in need, maybe even someone close to you."

I didn't realize it then, but in some way he was trying to tell me about what was going on in Sudan. He never talked about the war, but when I wouldn't listen to his stories about the orphans he would say, "Listen, my boy. You think you are safe, that this society will always love you. But this society is corrupted. When you grow up, you need to help people. Don't be selfish."

It was not until years later that I learned what my dad had been telling me about orphans was not just to prepare me for my future. He had spent much of his time in the city taking care of orphaned children. Though he was not educated, he made good money in the city, so he used his money to send orphaned children to school.

It wasn't until many years later, in one of the refugee camps in fact, that I found this out from an old friend of Dad's who recognized my name, and told me the story about how my father had helped the orphans.

Okay, so you grew up in South Sudan, in a little village, and you were orphaned as a young child. Yet you really made something out of nothing. So what was that first time you got a sense that you could do something? That you could make something happen?

The first time that I realized I could make something happen was in 1996, when I didn't even know how to write. I was 10 years old.

One morning I sat down on the curb, thinking about where my life was going. Children who were lucky enough to have parents rushed past me to the school. It was a primary school, and was about a 10-minute walk from where I was living. They ate cookies made by their parents as they made their way towards the school. As I sat and watched the kids go by with big smiling faces, acting as if they owned the whole world, I decided that I too would go to school, and that I too would have a good way of life some day. I figured that there must be something at school that was making the children so happy. It was in this moment, though I didn't know it at the time, I began to realize just how valuable education is, and the importance that every child should have the chance to go to school.

On the first day that I arrived at school, I was naked. All the other children were dressed. The headmaster introduced himself, asked me for me name, and said, "Mister Garang, where are your clothes?" So even going to school was harder than I had expected.

The school itself was very modest, fashioned in the same way that the houses were, out of mud and sticks. Unlike the houses, though, which were built to withstand the rain and the annual flooding of the Nile, the schools were not given the same attention. They were made with smaller trees and a lot of mud. As it was a public school, it was in the poorest of conditions: there were seats for the teachers and students crafted out of mud, and a blackboard. We wrote with our exercise books balanced on our laps.

I was in the school, looking at the other kids. Some were orphans, but some were not orphans. Some of them were having a hard time, but I was having a harder time than them, because they were better off than me. But I looked at them and said, "Oh my god, I really can't help this kid when I cannot even help myself."

So that was when I got the idea that, when I grow up, it did not matter whether I was wealthy or not, I was going to do something to help these people.

So you went through this amazing journey in which you made your way to a refugee camp in Kenya. And there you were the beneficiary of a non-profit foundation yourself, weren't you?

Yes. After a few months in the refugee camp while I was working as an adult educator at a near-by school, I got lucky. A young man from Washington D.C. came to the camp to do an internship. His name was Vicrum Puri, and I met him during a general staff meeting. When he was introduced to us, he stood up and spoke about where he was from. After the meeting, I approached him and spoke more about where he was from and finally explained my situation to him. I asked him if he or someone he knew could help sponsor me to go to college. He looked down at his feet, and said with a soft voice, "I will think about it, Peter. I have to talk to my dad first."

His father's foundation, the DD Puri Foundation, is a small enterprise based in Washington D.C., which helps students in Africa and the South Pacific afford to attend school. There were a lot of students that he, like my dad before me, wanted to help, but there was no way that his foundation could help them all. I was able to prove to him that I was dedicated and worth his while, and the DD Puri Foundation ended up paying for me to attend college in Eldoret, Kenya and for my semester at the Community College of Vermont.

So you came to Vermont and you started working on a business degree—when

did it occur to you that you wanted to find ways to start helping your community in South Sudan?

The first thing that came to my mind was not actually to do what I am doing now, helping orphan kids. Instead, I was looking around, and I was seeing the widows whose husbands had been killed in the war, or had died prematurely. And I said, well, I need to help these women really have a better life. But when I had gained an education in the United States and I was finally in a position to do something for my people in South Sudan, I realized that I could not speak from experience—from these widows' experience. So I said well, I'd better do something in the future to help the orphan kids, because I really know what they're facing, and I experienced it myself. I know how it works, to be an orphan child. So, if I can put that bad experience to good use that would really make more sense.

In 2005, when I went back home and met with a group of young orphan kids, that's when I almost cried. That's when I went and looked at this kid and said to myself, "Well, I don't have anything to help them, but with God's power, I will definitely do something about them." So I promised them at that point what seemed to be an empty promise to me, because I didn't know that I was really going to be able to keep it. But I did promise them anyway that I would come back and so, five years later, this is what I'm doing. One of them now is a student of the foundation that I run.

So your way of helping these orphan children, back in your homeland of Sudan, is to raise money in the States, so that you can pay their tuition and expenses to attend school. And what are some of the tools that you learned, the skills, the knowledge that you learned that have helped you to do that?

Be myself, and be able to give a good speech, talk to people in a nice way, get the word out to people so that when I talk to someone I feel confident that that person is going to send a check.

And then another thing was networking.

Networking is very challenging to do when you are new to this country, and you don't know anybody, so you just have to go and introduce yourself to them. It isn't easy to say, "I am from Sudan, and part of this organization here, and it is nice to meet you, and this is why I'm running this foundation." It is tricky because every time people see you greeting them, they know, "This guy is going to ask for money."

How do you think you gained the self-confidence to do that? You get right in there and introduce yourself, and speak up. Where do you think that came from?

One source could be the inner wisdom that I have, that I don't think I learned from people. Another thing is the encouragement from people, people like the chairman of my foundation telling me, "Go there and get the word out!" So I'll say, well, I don't want to let people down. All of this, put together, gives me this power to say, "Yes, I can do it! If that person can do it, why not me?"

So you used a very interesting expression there, your "inner wisdom." Talk about your inner wisdom.

Well, every time I want to do something, my inner wisdom tells me whether it is right for me to do. It means I don't really feel any fear, like when I stood up in front of 100 people. I wanted to say something, and I said it with the confidence that these people were going to leave with a full understanding of what I was talking about. I would say that I was born literally as a speaker. Another part of my inner wisdom is that if I'm meeting with a person who is new to me, something tells me, "This person, you have met him or her before." And I will talk to that person as if I have known him or her for years. So that is part of my inner wisdom, and part of my inner wisdom is that when I sit down at a time of difficulties, I feel that there is nothing difficult to overcome.

Is that because you've had so much difficulty in the past? Nothing seems really bad?

Yes, these difficulties are nothing compared with

all of the things that I went through when I was a child. At this point, people are still wondering—people who knew me when I was five years old—how this young boy overcame all these challenges. That gave me the power to say, "Well, if I overcame all those challenges, then why not overcome this challenge then?"

▸▸

Peter persuaded me to join his board of directors, and after a year and a half of operation under his leadership, we have made good progress. Currently, NSJOF funds the education of seven orphan children at private schools in Uganda. Most of the money has been raised through Peter telling his story to interested groups and individuals. His book, *Lost Generation: The Story of a Sudanese Orphan*, has helped tremendously (available on Lulu.com). Peter has had to dramatically improve his English language and public speaking skills.

After graduation from Champlain in May 2011,

Peter took a job helping two local school districts improve their outreach and service to the area's growing refugee/immigrant population. Over the summer, we continued to meet on a regular basis and he updated me on his progress with his work. Then, in August, he dropped a bombshell. He had a new venture in mind, a bold venture which, if successful, will transform the scope of NSJOF's impact and dramatically change the trajectory of Peter's life.

He pointed at the laptop on my desk and invited me to google "Peter Eagle Transportation Company." I did, and was amazed by what came up: an almost fully functioning website promoting what I soon learned was Peter's latest venture. Peter Eagle Transportation was being established to provide "American" coach-style bus service to the people in the smaller cities and towns of East Africa. What does "American" style service mean? To Peter, that means clean, reliable buses, no one standing in the aisles, a bottle of water and snacks served to each passenger en route. We reviewed his cost structure, margin expectations and some management control, operational and marketing issues. Everything seemed reasonably well thought out.

He told me that his plan was to give a significant ownership share in the new company to NSJOF so that the Foundation's growth and stability would be ensured. He was starting to raise capital and wondered how to approach American investors. My first reaction to that question was that Peter would need to reassure investors that he could manage the corruption that was rampant in many of these countries, as it could rob his company of any profit potential and make running it unbearable. I suggested he research the scope and nature of corruption in these countries so he could formulate strategies to address the problem. The CIA, the U.S. State Department, and the United Nations all published extensive information on the business climate in countries around the world. That would be a good start.

I didn't see Peter for several weeks but the next time I saw him his smile was even larger than normal. I've learned to expect the unexpected from him, and he did not disappoint. "Guess what?" he exclaimed. "We have bought our first bus. It started running on Tuesday—full, no problems." I learned later there was one problem, but Peter had been able to secure a good lawyer and solve it satisfactorily.

He had a trusted friend and fellow tribesman from his days in school in the refugee camp watching operations of the bus company. He decided to forego the more ambitious capital raising he had originally contemplated and "bootstrap" the company instead. He took some of his own savings and raised the rest of the approximately $15,000 from trusted friends and members of the Sudanese community in Burlington. This capital was the level necessary to buy the first bus, a smaller bus than originally planned, and cover start-up working capital. He was off and running and his bus was running full, and making profit margin goals. His customers were happy, very happy—and Peter was planning for his second and third and fourth bus.

Within his story, which he tells in his book, one finds many of the attributes of successful entrepreneurs—the undying optimism in the face of horrific challenges, the instinct to reach out, to network, to find people—total strangers—to help him along the way, his curiosity and thirst for knowledge, his perseverance in the face of what to most of us would be insurmountable obstacles, his ability to focus on what is important. They are all there.

What does the future hold for Peter? It is hard to say. My feeling is that he will be inexorably drawn back to South Sudan to help the country rebuild and to help his people realize their potential, as he is clearly doing.

FINAL STORIES, THOUGHTS & ENCOURAGEMENT RB

How do I wrap this book up? What more can I do to help or encourage you, the reader of these stories, as a young person who may already be thinking of starting some new enterprise or project, something entirely your own?

For a start, I can reassure you that you're not alone in that ambition. I have a hard drive full of other interviews with students telling stories of their adventures in entrepreneurship.

There's Jade Jenny, a 2010 summa cum laude business graduate, who developed plans to open a CrossFit fitness studio while in BYOBiz. He raised $50,000 in capital during his final semester, then used a blog and social media to open his doors three months later with 60 percent of his capacity filled. His business turned cash positive after four months of operation, and Jade recently celebrated the first anniversary of Champlain Valley CrossFit by negotiating a lease for significantly larger space.

In high school, Peter Jewett (Business '07) used his self-taught web development skills to start several cash-producing businesses. At college he sold his ski racing buddies' used skis on eBay and turned that into a thriving eBay services company. After tiring of dealing with a warehouse full of other people's stuff for sale, Peter borrowed a concept from super-fast-growing Burlington web services company Dealer.com, to create a web/marketing services company targeting mattress retailers.

When Max Murray (Business '12) was seventeen, he was running his own landscaping/excavation company with several adult employees. At Champlain, Max has combined his passion for heavy equipment with his interest and experience in the ski business to create Mountain Ventures LLC, a consulting company that helps small- to medium-sized ski resorts optimize the efficiency of their mountain operations: snowmaking, grooming, staffing. His work took him to British Columbia two summers ago to work with a ski resort to develop a snowcat skiing operation to complement resorts's lift-serviced facilities.

Then there is freshman Joshua Cohen (Communications '15), also known as DJ StereoShock, a composer and producer of electronic dance music. In addition to working on his music, Joshua is focused on building DJ StereoShock into a global brand. His music is played internationally in clubs and on digital radio. His only lament at the moment is that at 18 he is too young to perform in most clubs in the United States.

Drew Iacovazzi (Business '11) worked for two years in BYOBiz on two different business ideas before he found and followed a passion for financial security. He gained significant experience through a series of internships, and this summer he started his first job post-graduation as Assistant to the CEO of a financial services firm in the Hartford area. He'll do well in his steady job, I am sure, but I am also sure that the entrepreneurial world has yet to see the last of Drew Iacovazzi.

But as I listen and re-listen to these young people relate their own adventures in entrepreneurship, I can see patterns, some of which may apply to you.

Most, if not all of them, were trying things on their own and accepting personal responsibility at an early age. Nick Foley cutting lawns, or Jon Fischer competing in statewide robotics competitions, or Peter Garang Deng simply trying to survive on his own, they all had responsibility early in life. I am not sure that any of them were conscious at the time that their taking personal responsibility was significant to their development as entrepreneurs, but it was. Do not be afraid or shy away from opportunities to take responsibility, to lead.

They have all been lucky to discover a passion, some for an activity, like music or snowboarding or writing, others for the sheer joy and sense of accomplishment that comes from seeing a business, your own business, take off and grow. I think the important thing here is that the passion was self-discovered. Parents may have introduced it in some cases, but in every case the student embraced it on their own terms. You never know where or when you are going to find your passion, so it all comes down to curiosity. How curious are you?

Some of these students realize that they are in some ways different from their peers, and struggle for a time with acceptance. Nick Foley describes well the conflict he felt for many years, between really enjoying and valuing the landscaping business he was building, and being haunted by feelings that he should "not be doing this" out of fear that he would not be accepted by his peers. Even in college, he still wonders if he should be working so hard on his business, something he

clearly loves and enjoys, or spending his time doing "what most other college kids do." It is interesting to me that at every turn, Nick decides in favor of his business. How would you decide?

All these entrepreneurs have learned to be very comfortable talking and relating to adults. Their experiences have enabled them to develop a self-confidence that will serve them well as they go forward. I can't stress this enough to young people. Do you take the time to talk to your parents' friends and other adults? Some will be boring, to be sure, but you won't know until you try.

Another aspect of all these stories is that the path these young people take is by no means linear. There are no straight lines, only twists and turns and surprises, opportunities that are either recognized, or not. A critical quality of successful entrepreneurs is the ability to recognize opportunity.

On the other hand, Molly and Ginger think they have found an opportunity—to stake out and claim a space in the emerging new world of multimedia cybercontent. Molly aspires to be a "tastemaker" for women who are into snowboarding and fashion, and Ginger is a coach and mentor to people dealing with serious chronic disease. Staking the claim to part of this new universe is the first part of realizing the opportunity. After that, for them, comes the challenge of building an audience and solidifying their position as the world is changing around them.

Speaking of opportunities, it is clear from their stories that the digital world has created boundless opportunities for today's young people. Not only for those on the technology side, but all those like Ginger, Molly, Nick, Jon, and even Peter with his buses in East Africa, who will use digitally based tools to enhance all kinds of business activity. If you think about it, time spent on Facebook, YouTube, Twitter, or a game console can be really valuable if you are taking the time to consider and understand the power of these tools. How well do you grasp this power?

A note about, and for, parents. The parents of most of the students featured in this book allowed and enabled their child to try something on his or her own. They were supportive, to be sure—but they gave their kids room to try things and even to fail. This is critical.

Finally, it is important to remember that all these stories are just the early chapters. So much lies ahead for all of these young people, and for you, the readers of this book. It dawned on me the other day that when I get to the point in my life when I am ready to retire (still a long way off, I hope), I will still be reading the unfolding chapters in all these wonderful stories–so let me say thanks in advance to all my students for adventures yet to come, and to another young entrepreneur, Mark Zuckerberg, for creating Facebook, which will surely make the task of following these adventures a lot easier.

ACKNOWLEDGMENTS

Let's get it right out on the table: this book would not exist without the vision, energy, and encouragement of my colleague Tim Brookes. That's Professor Tim Brookes, the unflappable Brit who runs Champlain College's Professional Writing Program and also founded Champlain Publishing, the ground breaking Champlain program which enables students to gain real-world experience working on real-life publishing projects for real life clients. Tim provided the wisdom and energy to see this project through. Tim also provided a full-blown publishing team made up of well trained Champlain students, who did much of the work of transcribing interviews, editing and re-editing chapters, designing layouts, securing photography, proofreading, and all the other important tasks that go into bringing a book idea to reality.

That team includes Champlain graduate Alli Neal, my indefatigable Project Manager, who led her team to get the project done on time and on budget. She also did a great job of managing me, which, as my wife will tell you, is no easy task. Jillian Towne, a senior Professional Writing major, and the managing editor for Champlain Publishing, did a great deal of editing and follow-up interviewing. John Wolfe, a junior Professional Writing major, took the lead transcribing the interviews and did some great investigative fact checking. Colleen Lloyd Sedlacek, a freshman Professional Writing major, also assisted in transcribing and copy-editing. The interior layout and design was done by Jordan LaCount, a senior Graphic Design major, who did a phenomenal job under phenomenal time constraints. The cover design came out of Professor Steve Craft's Projects in Graphic Design class. The chosen design was by senior Graphic Design major Kaitlyn Bouchard. Although not part of the assignment, the class also chipped in the title Outside the Box, having summarily rejected the working title that Tim and I had latched on to. My thanks also go to Queen City Printers for their support of the project.

Of course, I would never have written the book if BYOBiz, Champlain College's innovative entrepreneurship program did not exist. Many people can share in the success of this program. First and foremost, Champlain's President David Finney, who dreamed up the idea of BYOBiz after hearing many many Champlain students tell him about their entrepreneurial pursuits during informal chats. Many Champlain people contributed to starting BYOBiz, but special

mention should be made of my colleagues David Binch, Greg Morgan, Moneer Greenbaum, Charlie Nagelschmidt, and to consultant Betsy Walkerman. My heartfelt thanks also goes to the deans and faculty of the college who have given me their unqualified support and encouragement as BYOBiz has developed, and to our Provost Robin Abramson, who has been a great supporter of BYOBiz and this project and helped me greatly in my transition to the academic world.

Finally, my special thanks goes to my dear family: my wife Nancy and children Stephanie, Robbie, and Jamie, who consistently followed up their initial incredulous reaction, "You're going to write a book?" with sincere words of support.

ABOUT THE AUTHOR Robert Bloch

Robert Bloch graduated from Cornell University with a BA in Government and, with a childhood friend, set off to start a magazine publishing business targeting college students. Though the venture was ultimately not successful, the experience left him hooked on business, and he earned an MBA from Harvard University. Bob began his first business career in Fortune 500 companies as the assistant product manager for a division of General Foods, emerging eight years later as the chief marketing officer of Four Seasons Hotels Ltd., and later as CMO for Marriott Hotels, Resorts and Suites, Inc. His second career led him to co-found two institutionally-backed entrepreneurial ventures. Bob embarked on his third career in 2007 when he joined Champlain College, where he mentors student entrepreneurs as the first full-time director of its pioneering BYOBiz entrepreneurship program. He is an active angel investor and serves on several boards. Bob enjoys motorcycling and other outdoor pursuits, and currently resides with his wife, Nancy, in Charlotte, Vermont.

ABOUT THE PUBLISHER Champlain Publishing

Champlain Publishing was created in order to engage as many of our students as possible in the field of publishing, whether as writers, editors, designers, artists, marketers, publicists, accountants, or web designers, and to give them a supervised educational experience that is creative, demanding, and applicable to the world they meet when they graduate.

Our mission is to be an active part of the great experiment that is contemporary publishing.

Tim Brookes
Editor-in-Chief

ChamplainCollegePublishing.com

Project Manager Allison Neal

Editorial Team Jillian Towne, John Wolfe, Colleen Lloyd Sedlacek

Cover Design Kaitlyn Bouchard

Interior Design and Layout Jordan LaCount

Additional Design Concepts Catherine Black, Justin Keskin

Copy-Editing Katherine Quimby Johnson

Additional copy-editing Jordan Babcock, Abigail Clark, Emma Crockett, Ashley DeFelice, Alexa Ercolano, Skyler Lendway, Sarah Lucia, Abigail Messick, Paul Oka, Amber Parker, Michael Sheerin, Amina Srna, Courtney Triola, John Wolfe

Design Conception Development Steve Crafts and the Projects in Design class